THE
BEAUTIFUL
COUNTRY

THE
BEAUTIFUL

Maine to Hawaii

COUNTRY

Text by Arnold Ehrlich

A Studio Book · The Viking Press · New York

Acknowledgments

Apart from the photographers and authors cited, special recognition is due to Bryan Holme, Director of Studio Books, who conceived this project with love and faith. And to Nicolas Ducrot and Julia Colmore for their untiring help and interest.

Gratitude is also due Magnum, Louis Mercier, Photo Researchers, Inc., and Rapho Guillaumette, Inc., for their valuable cooperation, and thanks to *Sports Illustrated* for their permission to reproduce the photograph of Waimea Bay in Plate 74.

CONTENTS

THE PHOTOGRAPHERS

LES BLACKLOCK
(Plates 43, 44, 47, 70, 71, 72)

ROBERT BORNEMAN
(Plate 14)

ALFRED EISENSTAEDT
(Plates 3, 5, 6, 25, 28, 29, 30, 31, 41, 48, 49)

ELLIOTT ERWITT
(Plate 26)

DOUGLAS FAULKNER
(Plate 32)

ARTHUR GRIFFIN
(Plate 9)

ERNST HAAS
(Plates 15, 45, 51, 57, 64, 66)

ESTHER HENDERSON
(Plates 7, 8, 35, 42, 52, 56, 62, 63, 68)

TOM HOLLYMAN
(Plate 21)

CHRISTOPHER HOLME
(Plate 2)

RONNY JAQUES
(Plate 22)

GEORGE E. JONES, III
(Plate 16)

JANE LATTA
(Plates 17, 18, 19, 20)

NEIL LEIFER
(Plate 74)

FRED MAROON
(Plate 27)

WAYNE MILLER
(Plate 75)

DON MORGAN
(Plate 65)

IRVIN L. OAKES
(Plates 23, 24)

ROBERT PHILLIPS
(Plate 54)

DAVID PLOWDEN
(Plates 10, 11, 36, 38, 40, 46, 50)

WINTER PRATHER
(Plate 37)

BERNARD G. SILBERSTEIN
(Plate 39)

BRADLEY SMITH
(Plate 34)

JOHN LEWIS STAGE
(Plates 1, 4, 13, 33, 53, 55, 58, 60, 61, 67, 69, 73)

DENNIS STOCK
(Plates 12, 59)

To the next generation, who will inherit
and, we hope, cherish, the American earth

INTRODUCTION

"Where can I go now? Where can I go, now, and visit nature undisturbed?"
—John James Audubon

Audubon's cry of the mid-nineteenth century is the full cry of the 1970s: Where can everyone go, in the great American continent, to lose himself in the depths of its natural abundance? The need for space, for solitude, nags at the heart of all who are in search of that most precious of all imperatives—privacy.

One of the United States' greatest blessings is a network of national parks and wilderness areas, but still the demand is for more and more. The message is not only to get out and clean up the environment—so encroached upon by industry, by housing developments (some well, some poorly designed), by junk yards, by neon signs and billboards—but to discover more of the country's natural beauty, to seek the roaming room that everyone's spirit and body demands.

In the seventies almost everyone, not only in America but the world over, wants to be able to be alone on a mountaintop, to commune with himself and with nature—if only for a few moments.

Despite the current anguish over the polluted state of the air in the cities and of rivers (in the country), much of America, unspoiled and ravishing, is still out there for the seeking, as many of the photographs in this book attest. Even as Americans rail against the vanishing of open space and beauty spots, visitors from Europe, the Near East, and the Far East arrive in droves and are enthralled with the vastness of the land, with the very wonders that Americans take for granted: the loveliness of New England, the Great Smokies, the endless plains, the grandeur of such rivers as the Missouri, the majestic Rockies, the fantasy shapes of Utah, the rocky swell of the Pacific coastline. It is a healthy reminder that through the eyes and feelings of visitors every generation of Americans must perforce re-discover the land's own natural gifts.

Americans tend to love "natural" nature best—lavish, rugged, tumultu-ous—wild forests and unclimbable mountains and trackless deserts, stretches of coastline with only the birds for companions. The fresh, the virgin, the unmanhandled is their pioneer inheritance; and their true heroes are the "first to get there"—Lewis and Clark, Major John Wesley Powell, Daniel Boone. The eyes of young and old are constantly turned west of the Mississippi; over there, just beyond that mountain, across that far river, lies the promised land.

John Steinbeck's word "westering"—with all its bittersweet elegy for the fact that there are no more mountains to cross, no more rivers to ford, nowhere to go beyond the golden strands of California—echoes Audubon's cry: "Where can I go now?" Well, to Alaska, say the plucky and the adventurous, and perhaps in that state—so much a part of the ice age—the future lies. America still has its share of dreamers, of idealists; perhaps never in its history has it had more of them.

A lot of country had to be explored, opened up, civilized before the West could yield its staggering panoramas, and it is the national legacy that for the asking everyone can enjoy both the austere simplicity of a Vermont village green and the tumbled ranges of the Cascades; the gay sight of boats sailing out of a Massachusetts harbor; the mangrove swamps of Florida's Everglades, and the lordly peaks of Colorado; an unsaddled horse suddenly glimpsed in a rolling meadow in Kentucky; the rhododendron bursting to life in the Smokies; the other world of the Louisiana bayous; the spooky shadows over the Painted Desert; the mighty gorge of the Columbia River; the geometric, marching files of corn and wheat on the endless prairies; the buffalo and elk and antelope still roaming in the Black Hills of South Da-kota; the eeriness of Death Valley and the rock-fringed coast of Maine. The country, as visitors keep reminding Americans, is a cornucopia of splendors.

The photographs in this book are the work of cameramen with a lov-ing eye for the shapes and contours of the vast landscape. The pictures speak for themselves. Many of the words that follow have been borrowed from the pages of *Holiday*, a magazine that has given many distinguished American writers an opportunity to voice their own minds about their native states. It is a tribute to their collective eloquence that the words are as fresh as when they were first set down on paper; and that, even now, their love for the land comes through as deep as it is undisguised.

Despite all the tumult over the condition of the environment, there is still a beautiful America out there for everyone to find, to discover, to cherish.

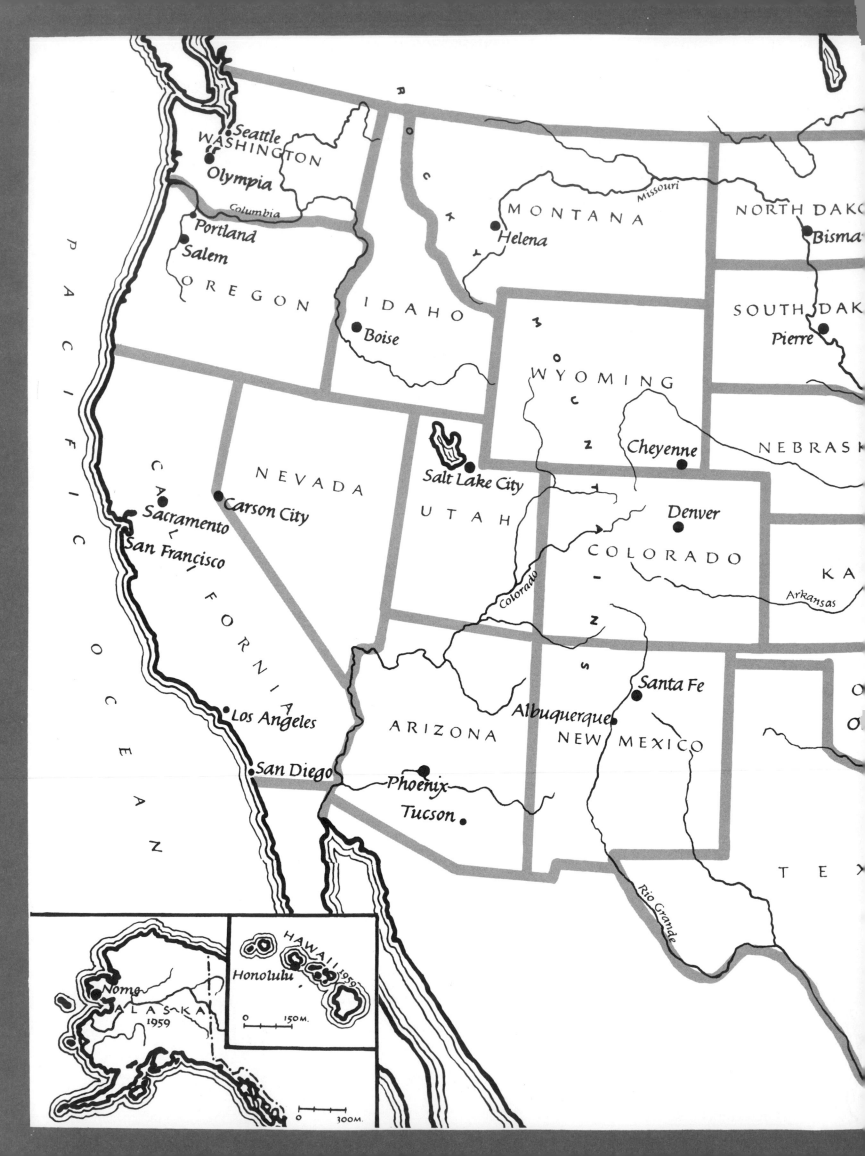

NEW ENGLAND

In a sense, New England is every American's spiritual home, whether his ancestors were original settlers or not, and it is therefore the national heritage, the newcomer's birthright as much as that of the nth descendant of a Pilgrim father. The late Bernard De Voto, historian, essayist, conservationist, a wise and gentle man, distilled the modern experience of New England:

"Endlessly misconceived, misrepresented, and even caricatured as New England has been, the most striking thing about it is this: no American ever comes here for the first time. Wherever he grew up, whoever his forebears were, he seems to bring with him something that could be called an ancestral memory except that, most likely, his ancestors never saw New England, either."

There is another characteristic of New England: ". . . a faint, evanescent feeling of personal recognition. Whether at first sight or after quite a while . . . the visitor frequently experiences a *déjà vu* of the heart. He seems to have been here before. He lived here a long time ago; some part of his boyhood was spent here. He had forgotten about it but now, in momentary glimpses of things gone before he can identify them, he seems to be beginning to remember. In some profound and subtle way he has come home."

Granted that the Currier and Ives image of New England is a thing of the past, it is remarkable how much New England still radiates the physical characteristics we most expect of this stern, first-settled corner of America. The clichés, the picture-postcard views, the artifacts are abundantly present, even now; and imagine our disappointment if we came to visit and found that they had evaporated. The village green surrounded by stately trees; the spire of the Congregational Church shining white against a clear blue sky; the striped lighthouse by the rocky, gull- and seal-haunted coast of Maine; the covered bridges; the hilly farms strewn with boulders; the old barns, red against the flaming autumn foliage; the ample white clapboard houses, their windows gleaming, their shutters fresh from a coat of black paint, or green. The forested hills, the granite mountains, the still ponds, the ever-surprising grandness of the lakes, the propinquity of the sea.

And then, too, the tradition-proud preparatory schools, the snobby colleges and universities, the forgivable (and sometimes laughable) superiority of encrusted values and cherished ideas. All of it poured as if from a hundred different paint tubes into a likeness that could emerge only as New England. And more—a certain style, a defined elegance in the very land itself that makes it acceptably, bearably *human*. What comes as a surprise, almost as a shock, is that all the foregoing elements *are* to be found there today.

New England, of course, shines greenly from spring into summer, and in the fall is transformed into a spectacular blaze of color. Then winter. Except for the skiers, nobody in his right mind would go beauty worshiping during the icy and snow-whipped winter months except to enjoy a white Christmas. A New England winter has a puritan, white-blanketed sternness that goes beyond prettiness, that silhouettes barn and house and stripped tree against a lowering sky with a harsh beauty peculiarly its own.

"Though the felicities of progress and sophistication have tempered the tyranny of the northern winter," writes novelist Jean Stafford, "it is still a challenging and heady time; it is not all a winter carnival and chic resorts. Away from the cities and away from the skiing centers, along the shores of Maine where the North Atlantic mightily decamps and in the farming lands of New Hampshire and Vermont, the winter has not lost its rigors; it is old-fashioned, it is hard, beautiful, solemn; it is a season of great character and living through it requires pride and stamina. The rewards of the struggle are bountiful: the eye is continually delighted and refreshed, the heart is eased by the imposition of simplicity upon it, the intellect admires the imperious rages of the elements and the Yankee refusal to be cowed by them."

One other generalization about New England before we consider its bill of particulars, what De Voto calls its "neatness, clarity, and precision that are true elegance. This elegance is the swept and garnished . . . countryside, the houses and town halls and meetinghouses whose white paint is spiritual dignity, the fanlights of the mansions, the scrubbed stoops (with a pumpkin on them at harvesttime) of the farmhouses, the farmhouses themselves, sited not only so that they are sheltered from the prevailing wind but so that they take in the vista of the creek curving toward the fold in the hills."

Maine

Our point of departure, the wild and beautiful upper reaches of the New England coast—two hundred and fifty miles from the Piscataqua River, where it begins, to the Bay of Fundy, where it ends. The New England coast has countless bays and coves, islands and rivers; it can be bleak, angry, baleful, serene; it can also be as sunny as the Mediterranean, but the swimming is never warm. There is also the suggestion of a majestic solitude—as at Pemaquid Point, whose lighthouse, supreme symbol of the seafaring life, is both a warning and a comfort.

Geologists call the Maine shoreline a "drowned coast," and today every island is a mountaintop. The coast actually splits into three parts: the Western Coast, from Kittery to Portland; the Middle Coast, from Portland to the region around Mount Desert Island; and the Eastern Coast—the true Down East—from Frenchman Bay north and east to Canada.

The Western Coast is the Maine of sandy beaches and artists' colonies; Winslow Homer painted these shores as thousands do today. Ogunquit in summer is a disturbed anthill, only sixty-five miles from Boston. Beyond Cape Elizabeth and Portland Head, the blue waters of Casco Bay and the spruce- and pine-filled Calendar Isles compose into the Maine of retreat and solitude. The Calendar Isles (less than half the year in number) are the first of several thousand mountaintops between here and the Bay of Fundy. Some of the smallest islands are still for sale.

One of the most noted Maine islands is Monhegan (reached by boat from Boothbay Harbor or Port Clyde), a small, cliffy, year-round home of lobster men and a haven for summer painters. Lobster—drawn fresh from these chilly waters, boiled (never broiled!) in sea water, served with melted butter with a dash of freshly ground pepper—a supreme dish on its native grounds, a rubbery concoction when frozen and heated.

Between Portland and Penobscot Bay, particularly at Wiscasset and Belfast, are the fine old white houses built by sea captains. Wiscasset is one type of New England village, a seafaring place and one of Maine's prettiest; a town of elegant eighteenth- and nineteenth-century houses built of brick and wood, with fanlights and widows' walks, tidy gardens and trimmed lawns, elms and evergreens. It is the rare driver who won't pause at Wiscasset, on U.S. 1, the busy lifeline of coastal Maine that rushes right through town. Nearby is Boothbay Harbor, and farther north, another special place to stop at and enjoy is Camden, with its long yacht harbor and backdrop of green hills.

Between Brunswick and Rockland the long, broken peninsulas extend from the mainland in fringes of gray and green. Off U.S. 1, beyond Bucksport, is the village of Castine—the New England of the trancelike dream, which still turns out blue-water captains from the Maine Maritime Academy's training ship, the *State of Maine*. This region is the Maine of coastal hills, ponds and inlets, and of peaceful villages—Penobscot, Brooksville, Sedgwick, Brooklin. Across Blue Hill Bay is Mount Desert and on Mount Desert Island is Bar Harbor, which since the fire of 1947 has never been quite the glamorous resort it once was. On the other side of the island, you can visit Seal Harbor and Northeast Harbor to watch the Rockefellers and Fords at summer play.

Beyond Cadillac Mountain, teeming Acadia National Park and knife-edged Schoodic Mountain, beyond the cove villages of Birch Harbor and Prospect Harbor and Corea, you are truly Down East, "east of Schoodic." Blueberry barrens, scrub oaks, flat gravelly soil; a haunted, dangerous coast of tides, fogs, whirlpools. Submarines cruise under the Arctic-like waters, the candy-striped lighthouse stands out against the green of Campobello Island, the sea is a gray-green, glassy deepness, and the jagged blue-black rocks are treacherous. This is American primitivism, stark and coldly beautiful.

And then there is inland Maine with its cities, Bangor and Augusta (the state capital); its farms, mountains, and almost countless lakes, large and small, encountered as you drive westward toward the White Mountains and New Hampshire, or turn north into the broad arc of the Canadian border.

"I never knew, or had forgotten how much of Maine sticks up like a thumb into Canada," John Steinbeck writes in his *Travels with Charley*. "We know so little of our own geography. Why, Maine extends northward almost to the mouth of the St. Lawrence, and its upper border is perhaps a hundred miles north of Quebec. . . . As I drove north through the little towns and the increasing forest rolling away to the horizon, the season changed quickly and out of all proportion. Perhaps it was my getting away from the steadying hand of the sea, and also perhaps I was getting very far north. The houses had a snow-beaten look, and many were crushed and deserted, driven to earth by the winters. Except in the towns there was evidence of a population which had once lived here and farmed and had its being and had then been driven out. The forests were marching back, and where farm wagons once had been only the big logging trucks rumbled along. And the game had come back, too; deer strayed on the roads and there were marks of bear."

Massachusetts

"Nowhere in the United States does the eye encounter a landscape more various and contrasting than in the postage-stamp cosmos of Massachusetts," wrote Henry Morton Robinson.

The state boasts two thousand miles of shoreline, thirteen hundred lakes and ponds, and innumerable brooks; prosperous farms, historic houses, churches, villages, and towns far too numerous to single out for mention; the lovely scenery of the Berkshires, tobacco fields, apple-laden orchards, and winding roads thick with antique shops. Its capital, Boston, is perhaps the last truly civilized city in America. Despite developers, the physical wealth of Massachusetts appears inexhaustible—eight thousand square miles of ever-changing patterns of weathered, established loveliness. It would take years to explore every corner of the state, and a lifetime to know Boston (and still you wouldn't be a part of it if your ancestors didn't come over on the *Mayflower*).

The Berkshires, the polarization of the sea-bent coastal areas, are the scenic uplands that rise in the northwest corner of the state. This Swiss-like land may, geographically, belong more to Vermont or Connecticut or even New York. The Berkshires are a segment, thirty miles long, of the rolling range that forms the Green Mountains in Vermont and the Litchfield Hills in Connecticut. Hundreds of miles of roller-coaster roads crisscross this country, which William Manchester describes as "a kind of Raintree County, all green and golden and shimmering in the past, a remote land of haunting landscape, lean New England rivers, chiming cowbells and general stores fragrant with the scent of spice and kerosene and calico." The celebrated tourist attractions—Tanglewood, Lenox, Ted Shawn's dance festival, and the modern theaters in Stockbridge and Williamstown—are set against a rustic background of prim village greens and white clapboard churches. Herman Melville called a summer day in the Berkshires "glowing and Byzantine," and Henry James, visiting Edith Wharton in these hills, remarked that the most beautiful combination of words in the English language was "summer afternoon."

The highest mountain in the Berkshires, Mt. Greylock, is only thirty-five hundred feet, but the vista south of Williamstown, with tower-topped Greylock in the distance, epitomizes this slightly rugged terrain with its three hundred trout streams and its wildlife: turtles, chipmunks, foxes, raccoons, and the occasional wildcat, to mention a few. Lichen-covered gravestones and abandoned orchards and tumbling stone walls contribute to the Berkshires' flinty charm. The summer-tourist invasion and its accompanying honky-tonk revelry never quite diminish the chief assets of the area, its rustic scenery and moving-about space for bird watchers, berry pickers, mushroomers, whittlers, and dedicated loafers.

Andover, Groton, Deerfield, and other impressively situated preparatory schools merit more than a passing glance; they are almost classical fixtures in the Massachusetts landscape. Old Sturbridge, halfway between Springfield and Worcester, is New England's equivalent of Williamsburg. It is an inventive and faithful recreation of a Colonial village of 1790, complete with old homes, barns, shops, mills, a general store and tavern, pillory and stocks, white Baptist Meeting House, and a handsome Mansion House, all carefully re-erected around an oblong village green.

On the coast, Salem, Gloucester, Marblehead still preserve much of the old-flavor charm of seafaring Massachusetts. And there is Plymouth with its rock, its *Mayflower* replica, and touristy ambiance. And, once more, Boston. The only way to see this Cretan labyrinth is patiently, on foot. From a top-floor room at the still-gracious Ritz Hotel overlooking the Common, the almost-changeless prospect of old Boston unfolds along with the new, one of the rare prospects that even hint at a sense of permanence in citified America. Across the Charles River is the stately grandeur of the nation's oldest university, Harvard, and its female counterpart, Radcliffe. And in suburban Jamaica Plain lies the 285-acre tract of the Harvard-controlled Arnold Arboretum where from April through May nature lovers watch a flowering spectacle of witch hazel, alder, birch catkins, Oriental cherry trees, crabapple, and lilac.

Back to the sea and those cluttered yet still appealing outposts, Cape Cod, Martha's Vineyard, Nantucket. The Cape is a magnificent arm of sand dune and scrub wilderness, such boisterous summer playgrounds as Provincetown, and serene retreats. At Woods Hole, science permeates the town in the form of marine and biological research. Cotuit, Osterville, and Wianno are Edwardian in their opulence, and Hyannis Port is too famous for comment. Wellfleet, in an area of woodland, freshwater ponds, and winding dirt roads, is Cape Cod at its least spoiled; and nearby Truro, Orleans, and Eastham lie in the serenest part of the Cape, a place of marshes and creeks and superb sand dunes and an entranced sense of peace as at the Cape Cod National Seashore.

At the heel of Cape Cod is Martha's Vineyard, a small island of lofty headlands, steep cliffs, unspoiled dunes, handsome houses in sailing-oriented Edgartown and Menemsha, where there is everywhere a feeling of wide horizons and the presence of the sea. Tiny Nantucket, only fifteen miles long and no more than three and a half miles wide, is one of New England's last holdouts against the developers: a mist of moors and dunes and scrub grass and ponds and mealy plum and cranberry bogs and grand whaling-captains' houses in Nantucket Town; and hundreds of small, unelaborate homes of a cedared shingle that ages into a silvery gray. It is an island of fogs and other mixed blessings of the sea—cooling in summer, raging and erosive in winter.

These neighboring New England states have always been conceived as a couple; or at least in the popular mind they are inseparably twinned. Well, yes and no. New Hampshire's mountains are stern, stony, and white; Vermont's are green, softer, more feminine. New Hampshire towns and cities, including Concord, the capital, have a prosperous, efficient appearance. Vermont's appear more muted, softer keyed, richer in texture. In the fall, Vermont foliage is a sea of blazing color, while the New Hampshire landscape is slightly less vivid.

New Hampshire Vermont

Perhaps the most memorable symbol of Vermont was Robert Frost, New England's poet laureate. One thinks of him leaning with ax in hand against a stand of birch trees on his rock-heaved farm in Ripton, in front of his weathered, two-story frame house. The simple rural images seem to echo the lyric humanism expressed in Frost's poems, the strongly felt love of this scaled, exquisite land.

The New Hampshire image is best seen in its tumbled White Mountains, where the New England profile achieves its aquiline summit. Mount Chocorua, often called the Matterhorn of America, lifts a stone face above its lake in a landscape of green and rocky openness, a masculine, virile composition.

Traveling down the Connecticut River, crossing and recrossing it, going from New Hampshire to Vermont and back again, is perhaps the best way to catch the feel of both. The river is New England's great waterway, the power that holds both states together, separating their differences, melding their likenesses. The Connecticut rises in northern New Hampshire, two hundred yards from the Canadian border, and empties 392 miles away into New York's Long Island Sound. At West Stewartstown, New Hampshire is separated from Vermont. At Newbury, Vermont, with its often-photographed red dairy barn, the river is at its loveliest. William Manchester refers to "her Sweet Afton mood. Drifts of goldenrod brighten the rippling meadows, red silos drowse in the afternoon sun. Along the valley's upper terraces, which rise as evenly as the layers of a caterer's cake, are elegant stands of elms, saltbox houses with wide-throated chimneys, and meetinghouse spires, vivid against the hills like white stilettos. In October the upper valley is exquisite. Pumpkins grin from farmhouse porches: for some reason the turning foliage is gold on the New Hampshire side and russet in Vermont—let botanists scoff, it *is*—and the water, unless crinkled by a breeze, faithfully reflects the colors of the bordering trees."

Near St. Johnsbury, Vermont, the spring air is sweet with the smell of evaporating maple-sugar sap. Revolutionary history crowds these banks—for example, Charlestown, New Hampshire, a grim outpost in Indian country, memorialized by Kenneth Roberts in *Northwest Passage*. The river towns—Lower Waterford, East Barnet, McIndoe Falls, Orford, Lyme—are quintessentially New England. At Hanover, Daniel Webster's Dartmouth College, a trim campus of neat white buildings, symbolizes New England's respect for classical learning and personal responsibility.

In the west rise Vermont's Green Mountains; in the east, New Hampshire's White Mountains; and the entire landscape crowding the river is satisfyingly pastoral. Soon the river flows on through Massachusetts and Connecticut. We will leave it here.

New Hampshire vignettes: The colonial town of Amherst, in the southwestern part of the state, has a pear-shaped common and the traditional steepled white meetinghouse.

A boulder on the common informs that this was the birthplace of Horace Greeley, whose advice to the youth of his day is still memorable: "Go West, young man, go West!" Mount Monadnock, a 3165-foot-high mound of granite, is worth climbing for a rolling panorama of hilltop farms, ponds, forests, and little villages nestling in the valleys. At Peterborough, the MacDowell colony still flourishes, with many unheralded writers in residence. The Cathedral of the Pines, on top of a knoll near Rindge, has a spectacular view of Mount Monadnock and neighboring lakes, valleys, and hills. Dublin, at 1485 feet above sea level, is the highest village in New England, the heart of the *Farmer's Almanac* country. Old-time New England is painstakingly preserved in Hancock, whose main street has scarcely changed in more than two hundred years. The white-pillared Hancock House is justly celebrated as one of New England's great inns.

In the Franconia Notch area, New Hampshire is as busy as Switzerland in the ski season. For the best view of "The Old Man of the Mountain," a craggy silhouette of a man's face formed by layers of granite and the state's most impressive sight, walk about two hundred yards along a brook to a boulder marker on the shore of tiny Profile Lake. The Kancamagus Highway, near Lincoln, provides thirty miles of travel through the wilderness of the White Mountains as the Indian knew it—the grandeur of silence broken only by the sounds of birds, wind, and water.

The Mount Washington railway takes one to the summit of New England, 6288 feet high, and from the top the glacial gouges in the landscape are evidence of a natural severity. From Moultonboro to Wolfeboro (sixteen miles), Lake Winnipesaukee, third largest in the country within a state's borders, stretches away like a great inland sea. This is the birthplace of the American summer resort, with 283 miles of shoreline, 274 islands, hills, and mountains that form a lovely (and terribly crowded) background. In Portsmouth, the first settlement in the state, many of the great homes of wealthy Colonial traders are still inhabited by their descendants, and a visit to the Governor Langdon House is an informative trip back to the eighteenth century. Not far away is New Castle, which—with its narrow, winding streets and houses flush with the curb—resembles an English fishing village.

Everywhere in New England the autumn is glorious, but nowhere is it more spectacular than in Vermont. Leaf watching in Vermont is a favorite fall weekend sport for thousands of New Yorkers and Bostonians, as well as for Vermonters driving out from the state capital, Montpelier, or from Burlington, its largest metropolis. The clogged state roads are frequently a nightmare, but autumn is the best time of the year to see nature at its most spectacular (a Vermont understatement!).

The mountain views from the Molly Stark Trail between Brattleboro and Bennington, particularly the Hundred Mile View at Hogback Mountain, are so magnificent as to seem unreal. Benedict Thielen writes, "The golden beech and elm leaves, the dark green of the unchanging firs and, above all, the hot scarlet and orange of the maples form a background you'll find nowhere else in the world."

Glass and pottery are in overwhelming abundance at the Bennington Historical Museum, and the tall trees of Old Bennington spread like torches above the white houses. In a countryside of handsome churches Bennington's Old First Church, "Vermont's Colonial Shrine," is one of the finest, and its cool gray-and-white interior is a miracle of restrained (but never austere) grace. The covered bridge—more than a hundred years old—at Sunderland, off the Ethan Allen Highway, is a photographer's imperative. Another splendid panoramic view is the Skyline Drive which leads to the top of Equinox Mountain. The countryside between fashionable Manchester and Rutland is the intense green of pasture, with the Green Mountains rising in the east above its span. This is cow country, brown and black-and-white clusters of cattle peaceably grazing in the fields, an integral part of the Vermont scene. Rutland and Proctor are good places to explore a native art, marble quarrying.

North of Middlebury, Vermont becomes wider and more open; on the other shore of Lake Champlain the Adirondacks rise in misty blue rows. Vergennes, incorporated in 1788, claims to be the smallest incorporated city in the country, and the intense blue paint on the scrollwork of many of its mansions lends a curiously gay air to the Victorianism of the town. Shelburne, near the shore of Lake Champlain, has what is surely the largest collection of Americana to be found anywhere, and the Shelburne Museum, twenty-five acres of reassembled old Vermont structures, displays the artifacts of America that delight antiquarians. Waterbury, Stowe, Smugglers Notch—this is Austria in Vermont; and the view from Mount Mansfield, the state's highest point, must surely satisfy even the most unappeasable hunger for leaf-turning at its October zenith.

From Middlesex to Stockbridge, along the Mad River, Vermont is wild, heavily wooded country. At Woodstock, the Rockefellers have refurbished the Woodstock Inn and in winter this is attractive ski country. Another superb inn (vintage 1793) is to be found at Newfane, an outstanding place to end a visit to Vermont. But before reaching Newfane, there is one last stretch of brilliantly shimmering scenery—the high country that rolls along with Vermont 8 below the restored village of Weston—a series of gold, orange, scarlet, and russet picture-postcard scenes that never tire the spirit.

Rhode Island Connecticut

The minuscules. Crowded, bustling, commuterized Connecticut still has many, many pockets of loveliness, but except in the north and northwest areas of the state, the wild is fast disappearing in the people- and industry-swollen tiny state squeezed between New York and Boston.

On the Long Island Sound side, Mystic (with its Mystic Seaport Museum) still displays its fine old whaling-captains' houses, and Groton and New London have a nice mariner's feeling, a submariner's jauntiness, and a pleasant tang of the iodine sea. Stonington is what everybody would wish Connecticut still to be, fierce rocky inlets and homes generously spaced apart. The Connecticut of Establishment wealth is seen in the manicured lawns and estates of Greenwich, and farther up, in New Canaan and Westport; and the fancy-pretty towns of Essex and Guilford still give this lowest part of the Connecticut River a towny, New Englandish charm.

The loveliest and most untouched part of the state is found in the northwest, around Sharon, the Cornwalls, Litchfield, Washington, Woodbury. The Housatonic Valley is a sloping region of hills (that rise into Massachusetts' Berkshire Mountains), of dense woods, and lakes, streams, and marshes where beavers still build their dams; and of drowsy farms where sleek Holsteins graze on rocky pastures dotted with wild flowers. It is the Connecticut of every disenchanted New Yorker's obsessive imagination.

Rhode Island is the state one zips through on the way from New York to Boston (or vice versa), yet such Narragansett Bay settlements as Wickford represent New England at its most retiring and shy and withdrawn. Also, this smallest state in the Union offers some of the pleasantest beaches and swimming in the East. Its sprawling capital is Providence. And the resort is Newport. The opulent, splashy grandeur, particularly in the turn-of-the-century white elephants along Newport's Cliff Walk, is often put down, yet this was once the seat of whatever aristocracy America could boast, the magnificent creation of booming wealth and giddy optimism, the marriage of American dreams with provincial vulgarity. It is a far cry from the tidy, prim, self-effacing New England. It is the America of Henry James versus the America of Robert Frost, and it is the measure of New England that it so successfully produced both.

THE MID-ATLANTIC STATES

This is the area—New York, Pennsylvania, New Jersey, Maryland, Delaware—that is as old as the Republic itself, muscular with industrial power, overweight in population, festering with run-down cities, yet still containing pockets of natural splendor that somehow manage to survive industrial and human cruelty.

From the Champlain valley in the north to the pretty little coves and inlets of the Chesapeake, the mid-Atlantic region is an area that still looks back on its Revolutionary and Civil War past. It is proud of its Federalist and Georgian architectural gems, yet is careless of the fate of its great rivers; it boasts magnificent woods and forests and mountains, yet is all too ready to succumb to the developer's wrecking ball. Possibly no region in America needs more the ministrations of the conservationist than these rich but used-up, beautiful but fast-fading dowager states of America.

New York

Of all the great natural wonders of the mid-Atlantic belt, probably the most singular spectacle is Niagara Falls (particularly the Horseshoe Falls, on the Canadian side) and the most encompassing one, the Adirondacks, one of the largest stretches of unspoiled country in one of the most beautiful regions of eastern America. To place it geographically, the Adirondack region is bounded by the Mohawk Valley on the south, the St. Lawrence Valley on the northwest, and the valley of Lake Champlain and Lake George on the east. It includes twelve New York counties in whole or in part; the Adirondack State Park, the largest state park in the country, more than twice as large as Yellowstone, covers 9,425 square miles and is somewhat larger than the state of Massachusetts. Once heavily forested, the Adirondack area, actually five distinct ranges lying almost parallel, is largely mountainous, with ninety summits rising above thirty-five hundred feet (the two most famous, Mount Marcy and Mount Whiteface, rise considerably over four thousand feet) and hundreds of lakes and ponds dotting the hilly terrain. Much of the Adirondacks is still true wilderness.

"An Adirondack mountain is thickly fir clad," writes Stephen Birmingham, "with a smoothly rounded top, but some offer steep slides, jagged cliffs, ledges, and tall rock-faced precipices with cascading waterfalls. At the feet of the mountains lie the lakes, many of them approachable only on foot, and a few that can be seen only from the air. From the valleys and lake shores below, the surrounding mountains form a stern horizon, dark green and brooding."

The Adirondacks woods are still full of spruce, balsam, hemlock, ash, cedar, and birch; trout and bass and pike and pickerel match wits with thousands of fishermen; deer flash through the trees. The wilderness, although no longer "forever wild," as the great conservationists of the 1890s hoped it would be, has enough primitive quality to bring lasting enjoyment to campers, sturdy hikers, walkers, sedentary nature lovers, or flower pickers.

Saranac, Lake George, Lake Placid, the Tupper Lake chain, are largely spoiled, but in the surrounding lonely woods and in those of Long Lake, Blue Mountain Lake, Raquette Lake, and the lakes of the Fulton chain there exists a backwoods feeling that repays the wanderer. The Ausable Chasm, overbilled as the "Grand Canyon of the East," is famed for its eroded, sculptured sandstone cliffs, two hundred feet high; and at the High Falls Gorge at Wilmington, the Ausable River drops more than a hundred feet over turbulent waterfalls.

The view of the entire Adirondack Forest Preserve is indeed moving from the summit of Whiteface Mountain; ferries ply Lake Champlain from New York to Vermont at three crossings. The stone fortress at Fort Ticonderoga is one of the great heritages of the colonial and Revolutionary Wars, and scattered through the six million acres of the Adirondack park are intelligent commercial attractions for children. They need not get bored in this semiwilderness, where, as Birmingham writes:

"In the evening stillness a whitetail deer pauses between the trees, then leaps into the shadow, his flag thrashing, disappearing like a passage of light across water. A black bear, moving like a clumsy ruffian, snuffs and paws about a deserted campsite. A red fox barks. A fish leaps and spanks the surface of the lake. In the underbrush a sinister shape moves; they say there are no more timberwolves here, but certainly some very wolflike creatures have been seen. As it grows darker, a wildcat rises from a branch and screams a scream to freeze the blood. The owl cries, and the rabbit cowers. Along the twilight trails the dead trees, where so many evil spirits stand imprisoned, reach out their fierce and craving arms." (The Adirondacks, once the roaming grounds of the warrior Algonquins, are still beautiful but, some say, also bedeviled.)

Carl Carmer once described New York as "a state of glinting waters," and the exquisite chain known as the Finger Lakes, lying between Lake Ontario's southern shore and Pennsylvania's northern border, support that simple but apt description. Their names are Canandaigua, Keuka, Seneca, Cayuga, Owasco, and Skaneateles. The rolling hills can be greener than Ireland in summer and the fertile valleys—this is wine country—bear such august Roman names as Ithaca, Sempronius, Cato, Ovid, Scipio, Romulus, and Marcellus. Rocky glens, ravines, hundreds of cascades—cataracts, splashers, ribbons—falls, and superb trout fishing in the tumbling streams offer outdoor recreation, in summer, at its healthiest.

Views? From the Sugar Hill Fire Tower west of Watkins Glen, Lake Ontario appears from one direction, and seventy-five miles away lies Pennsylvania. From the Bluff Point overlook at Keuka Lake, the Finger Lakes truly glint, and at Letchworth State Park, on the western rim, a seventeen-mile-long, six-hundred-foot-deep gorge with three waterfalls presents a staggering composition. Another and shorter gorge, at Watkins Glen, unleashes *nineteen* waterfalls. The wine country, almost Rhine-like in appearance and ambiance, is mostly centered in the mauve hills around Keuka and Canandaigua Lakes, and at Hammondsport and Naples the aroma of grapes can be pleasantly thick and heady. This is peaceful, controlled, yet thrilling countryside.

Equally worth exploring is what remains of the historic Mohawk Valley, with its strong and romantic associations of Indians and the early white settlers, and its contiguous unfolding with the legend-ridden Erie Canal. The Catskills, on the other hand, despite their frivolous identification as the Borscht Circuit, is somewhat surprising country, especially in the sparsely settled Rip Van Winkle region on the western side of the lordly Hudson River, replete with lovely trout streams and falls and windswept mountains. Frank Norris sums up: "The Indians called the Catskills the Land in the Sky, and that may sound pretentious until you come to realize that the Indians were not talking about altitudes, but about the rich quality of the sky itself which settles down upon these mountains. The sky always seems to be low in the Catskills, reflecting down and refracting back at any season the ochre and silver, vermilion and lime and gold of the rolling foliage beneath."

Sooner or later nearly everyone in his travels comes to, or passes through, New York City—no natural wonder yet certainly one of the seven man-made wonders of the modern world; a forest of steel, concrete, and glass. It is a city that is both heaven and hell, an American fantasy. Of the city's perverse and maddening beauty, E. B. White, in his classic *Here Is New York*, writes: "Manhattan has been compelled to expand skyward because of the absence of any other direction in which to grow. This, more than any other thing, is responsible for its physical majesty. It is to the nation what the white church spire is to the village—the visible symbol of aspiration and faith, the white plume saying that the way is up." Coming in from Queens on a summer morning, the traveler "looks southwest to where the morning light strikes the steel peaks of midtown, and he sees its upward thrust unmistakable: the great walls and towers rising, the smoke rising, the heat not yet rising, and hopes and ferments of so many awakening millions rising—this vigorous spear that presses heaven hard." But probably New York's most beautiful moment is in the blue of twilight, when the windows of its skyscrapers come alight and Manhattan (from across the East River or the Hudson) takes on an unequaled magic quality.

Pennsylvania

Penn's green and lush woods. To the native, this is the state that has it all, the bountiful and appointed place, the rich and fruitful land. Conrad Richter, a local man and writer, claims that he has heard more than one Pennsylvanian say on returning from a trip, "I've driven six or seven thousand miles and seen a lot of country, but nothing half so pretty as what we've got right here." Pennsylvania chauvinism is small-scale and insular, nothing like the raw boasting of the West.

What is peculiar about the state is that the nation is largely ignorant of its qualities; only the Pennsylvania Dutch country, its plague of tourist locusts and overphotographed quaintness, is at all generally recognizable. And most Americans seem to have a vague idea that Independence Hall, that jewel-like building of almost stark simplicity, is located somewhere in Old Philadelphia—but where? (Answer: Independence Square, between Fifth and Sixth on Chestnut.)

Millions of Easterners, let alone Westerners, are only dimly aware that forty miles due west of the Hudson River, Pennsylvania's own river, the Delaware, skirts the edge of a wilderness: the Great Highlands, which include the Lake Country, the Poconos, the Endless Mountains, the Black forests, the Seneca Highlands, and the Allegheny National Forest in the Upper Alleghenies—four hundred miles of frontier and solitude and often-wild beauty. How little these names are known: the Sawkill Creek, which rushes over a slab of rock into a forested gorge, then plunges into a deep chasm edged with rhododendron growing wild and laurel; Lake Wallenpaupack, fifty-two miles of shore line, clear, blue, forest surrounded; Penn's Woods, forest-covered mountains west of Scranton, stately, uniform rows of ridges that break up north of the Susquehanna into a forested maze barrier through which the early settlers hacked their way westward and gave the name that still stands: the Endless Mountains.

Pennsylvania has a mini-Grand Canyon, a gorge fifty miles long and a thousand feet deep, high up in the mountains of Tioga County near Pine Creek. At Coudersport, in Potter County, a miniature Black Forest appears, with black bears still prowling the denseness and an abundance of wild turkey. West of Kane, in the Allegheny National Forest, established by President Coolidge in 1923, there are seventy-four thousand acres —and all unknown—of unbelievably tall pines and hardwoods and hemlock.

Between the Pennsylvania Turnpike in the south and Route 6 in the north lies a huge strip of wilderness that remains practically unchanged since the first settlers arrived, an inner frontier of natural wildness called the Juniata Highlands. In southwestern Pennsylvania, the Laurel Highlands, an area of rich plateaus and Swiss-like mountains, red-and-white barns and flaming maples that was once America's western frontier, are the year-round playgrounds for the extroverted people of Pittsburgh. Better known to all, of course, is the poignant beauty of Gettysburg with its Civil War monuments and cannons along the old battle lines that strike every visitor dumb with awe.

Many people seem to forget that Philadelphia was the nation's first capital. The city—referred to often as the Florence of America—has some of the most attractive old houses in rows (around Rittenhouse Square, and again in reconstructed Society Hill), Georgian and Greek Revival public buildings, and notable art collections (private as well as in museums) in the entire country. And also, along the Suburban Main Line, it has some of the most photogenic estates.

Circling Philadelphia like a necklace are the counties of Bucks, Montgomery, Chester, and Delaware—old and beautiful regions, expensive farm country, with weather-resistant stone houses, superbly kept old Colonial estates, white-water streams, and (toward the Delaware River) low mountains and peaceful woods.

The charms of Lancaster County and its stubborn Amish flavor are, curiously enough, still authentic. The precisely planted soil, the clean barns with their decorative hex signs, the horse-and-buggy country roads, the bountiful farm tables, the entire air of satisfying but unsmug prosperity and cleanliness and simple living give the Amish country (some people call it the Pennsylvania Dutch country, others say Pennsylvania German country) a perennial and deserving appeal. The "peculiar people" have made much of eastern Pennsylvania—around Intercourse, for example—into a ravishing countryside where old ways and productive love of this fruitful soil abide.

Pennsylvania, a mountainous and forested state, a topographically jumbled land more varied and endowed than many small nations, encompasses everything from the fixed stillness of Valley Forge to the oak-bordered sands of Lake Erie. Alistair Cooke claims that at Azilum on the Susquehanna there is the noblest view in the East. From the Poconos in the east westward to the Alleghenies, Pennsylvania is a state of constantly surprising natural quality. And, near the western boundary, industrial Pittsburgh stands as the southern gateway to Ohio, the Easterner's first glimpse of the Midwest.

New Jersey Delaware Maryland

Dominated by their neighbor giants, these three small states fill out the Middle Atlantic belt. Taking the last first, Maryland, which claims to have the most individual character of the three—a unique blend of North and South—here is what author James Warner Bellah says:

"Two-thirds of Maryland is tidewater. For thirty-two miles of Worcester County the open Atlantic pounds the outer Maryland shore. West from the ocean the creek-laced Eastern shore spreads its low and fertile acres to the Chesapeake Bay, a broad land-bound sea that divides the state in twain. West from the Chesapeake the land rises at once, breaks into intermediate rolling valleys and rises again toward the Appalachian Range, which spines the western reaches of Maryland. But before the Appalachians are reached one must traverse the great valley of Washington County. About thirty miles long and twenty wide, this valley is as magnificent in scenery as the storied Shenandoah and as productive as any soil in the world."

The best of Maryland, or rather most of the best, is found on the Eastern Shore —Talbot and Queen Annes counties, long, narrow peninsulas surrounded by water; and English-sounding places such as Easton, St. Michael's, Tilghman, Oxford, and Cambridge with their wide creeks, rivers, and bays. This is crab-and-oyster country and also a place where individualists seem wedded to the water, a place where many attractive old homes retain their wide lawns and colonial seafaring atmosphere.

25

The shoreline of New Jersey, on the other hand, is not the place to look for beautiful America; and except at Cape May, the oldest seashore resort in the country that has managed to retain a well-kept and balanced atmosphere, the Jersey coast is a raucous, overcrowded stretch with good swimming nevertheless.

But the Delaware Water Gap in the northwest, where New Jersey, Pennsylvania, and New York join, still merits its reputation as "picturesque." The rolling countryside and many lakes are a pleasant relief from the flatness of the vegetable-growing areas of the "Garden State."

Morristown, some thirty miles distant from New York City, boasts one of General Washington's headquarters and a beautiful woodland park maintained around battlefields on which American history was made. And beyond Morristown to Far Hills, Bedminster, and Oldwick, New Jersey's rolling hill country—with its farm and woodland, estate and hunting areas—are roads that still lead off into eddies of quiet, unspoiled land.

Princeton, certainly one of the pleasantest university towns in the country, is a short drive from Trenton, the state capital. And so, in another direction—along the Delaware River, near the well-marked point where Washington crossed it—is Lambertville, reaching across the bridge to join New Hope in Pennsylvania. This artists' colony, with quaint buildings, streets, shops, and pretty surrounding country, is within a comfortable two-hour drive from New York, less from Philadelphia.

Possibly the state's least-known, but rewarding, attraction is the Wharton Tract, one hundred fifty square miles of forest located in the piney area of south central New Jersey. The Batsto Village restoration shows New Jersey life and artifacts of the period during 1776 to 1850, and a canoe trip through the many miles of winding streams is a mild but enjoyable trip through a wilderness that is as virgin as it was in the days of Washington and the Redcoats.

Delaware, too, has its coastline, the river from which it takes its name, lovely rolling hills, and flat and fruitful plains of staggering yield. Thomas Jefferson once called Delaware the "Diamond State," the reference being to the character of its citizens. Delaware troops have always been known as the Blue Hen's Chickens, because of the fighting cocks that native troops took into battle during the Indian Colonial Wars.

Perhaps because of the pervasive influence of the Du Ponts, Delaware could also be called the "Powder State," gunpowder being the original source of that family's fortune.

James Warner Bellah epitomizes tiny Delaware in this fragment: "A small but fiercely prideful state with the faint cavalier and bond-servant shadow of Virginia upon its beginnings, a kinship with Maryland's delightful Eastern Shore, the ponderous heritage of Penn's hardheaded Roundheads—a touch of the Dutch, a lacing of Scandinavian, a broad overlay of Scotch, Irish, and English, and a self-determined independence of thought and political entity that has given Delaware character and its people individuality for almost three centuries. And still does, in three small counties a hundred and ten miles in overall length, by nine miles wide at its narrowest and thirty-five at its widest."

The great Du Pont mansion, Winterthur, near Wilmington, Delaware's commercial center, opens its doors daily to a public eager to see only the best of America's antiques; and the acres and acres of park land surrounding this house-turned-into-museum are a joy, particularly in the spring. Other landmarks are Dover and New Castle, with their pleasant eighteenth-century buildings and general air of elegance.

THE SOUTH

Everything below the Potomac River, west of the Atlantic Ocean, east of Texas, and north of the Florida Keys is "the South." But traditionally it encompasses the eleven states that once comprised the Confederacy. Containing, in Virginia, at Jamestown, the first permanent English settlement in America, the South is as historic and rooted in its customs as New England.

Geologically, the South is very different from the land of the Puritans, yet it is equally varied—and beautiful. Romantic? Of course, if you think of Virginia's showy red-brick mansions and eighteenth-century gardens; or of Kentucky's rolling bluegrass pastures; or of the great Mississippi River; or of those famed antebellum houses, the white Greek Revival gems at Natchez or on out of New Orleans and New Iberia; and plantations approached through dreamlike avenues of gray-green lichen-laden trees. But not all of it is that. There are modern cities, industrial areas, slums, crowded vacation spots, just as there are almost everywhere in America today.

The South traces its cultural ancestry not only to the English, but to the Spanish. Take a look at Florida's restorations in St. Augustine, and to the French in Louisiana, centered in New Orleans. And, luckily, it is not without Indian remains. There is rich land, poor land, high land, low land, hillbilly land, and fur-trapper land; and splendid lakes. Dazzling acres of rhododendron, azalea, camellia, and magnolia contrast with those other stretches of Southern earth, the hard-worked, sweated-over fields of rice, cotton, and tobacco. Different again are the bayous, the swamps; the peach-tree orchards of Georgia; the citrus groves and flat truck gardens of Florida where fruit and vegetables are grown for the winter markets up North.

The mountains: the most spectacular are the Blue Ridge, the Allegheny range, the Great Smokies, and the Appalachians. The beaches: white sand stretches all the way down from Virginia Beach to Florida's tip and up again, concavely, to form the Gulf Coast; and in this popular ring of warm blue water, everywhere, still, there is room to swim. Wildlife: it is plentiful and exotic. Tangled swamplands, boggy bayous and conservation areas shelter egrets, hummingbirds, flamingos, deer, alligators. The weather: humid summers; mild winters in the north and warmer and warmer the farther south you go. Food: the freshest of fruit; fried chicken, shrimp creole, swordfish—and of course hominy grits comes with nearly everything you order.

The South geographically begins at Washington, the nation's capital, a place indisputably more Southern than Northern, with its soft foliage, grandiose Federal buildings; its traditional quality of stately courtliness in manners (sometimes abused, but where isn't it today?); its air of power and urgency, its cast-iron statues of military heroes, its long, hot, somnolent summer.

The city is at its most handsome during the short spring, after the Japanese cherry trees girdling the Tidal Basin burst out in blossom, and the air turns warm and soft and the parks and squares are carpeted in green. The grand monuments—the Jefferson Memorial, the Lincoln Memorial, the marble shaft commemorating Washington, the White House—always seem fresh and glowing after the wind-whipped, sooty winter; and the city itself seems renewed, anxious again to show itself off as the Federal capital.

Spring is the time of the great tourist invasion when thousands of high-school seniors pour in, camera at the ready, to check on their inheritance before graduation;

to see Washington in the full measure of its beauty, Washington in the springtime of its romantic appeal. One can already smell the South, in residential Georgetown especially and, of course, directly across the Potomac, where Virginia begins.

Virginia

The state that its partisans claim to be the most haunted by ghosts and the most consistently beautiful of all the states of the Union. Is there another state that more tenaciously remembers its past?

Virginia reveres its old buildings—Mount Vernon (commanding a magnificent sweep of the Potomac's estuary, where now and then a bald eagle—literally!—may drift by from the nearby promontory of Mason's Neck), Gunston Hall, and Woodlawn Plantation where there are always, in the prose of Charlton Ogburn, Jr., "Beauty and ghosts: these are the properties of the old houses, early or late Georgian and antebellum, of mellowed brick or white clapboard, that are scattered all over Virginia except in the extreme west. Many still belong to the families that built them generations ago: 'Keep it in the family' is a Virginian ideal."

The famous hunt country that extends from Leesburg, Middleburg, and Warrenton south to Charlottesville is actually part of the Piedmont. Ogburn describes it as "bolding rolling country, of meadowlands and woods with tree-lined streams, [that] combines views of far hills that lift the spirit with a sense of space and closed-in dales that comfort it with a sense of home. The Virginia Piedmont comes as near as any landscape could to the Arcadian idyll that has touched men's dreams since the day of the Greek pastoral poets." Has any state ever received a more fervent tribute from a non-native?

From its eastern to its western tip Virginia measures five hundred miles. Its westernmost point is actually twenty-five miles *west* of Detroit, and three-fifths of the Old Dominion are in woods: the evergreen of pine, mountain laurel, and holly and rhododendron; autumn sees the wild coloring of Virginia creeper, sumac, dogwood, and black tupelo. From Washington to Richmond lie the old blood-soaked battlefields—Fredericksburg, Chancellorsville, the Wilderness, Spotsylvania Courthouse—and the deserted roads and somber, pine-filled forests have a forbidding presence.

Beyond Richmond, the grand plantations of the James River and the eighteenth-century mansions of Shirley, Westover, and Berkeley show off Virginia at its most elegant. Virginians believe the plantation house of Carter's Grove is the most beautiful dwelling in the nation. Perhaps it is, but the competition is keen. Jamestown itself is sadly without charm, but the rolling green meadowland of Yorktown battlefield, high above the York River, commands a noble vista.

Of Colonial Williamsburg, one of the best-known tourist sights in America, little more can be said except that every traveler should stop once to wander among its one hundred and fifty or more buildings and well-tended gardens, and watch the artisans ply their almost-forgotten crafts and taste the place for himself. Artifice or the stirring recovery of a charming town? Only personal taste can say.

Watery Virginia, the Virginia littoral surrounding the Chesapeake Bay, is a felicitous region of sand beaches and marshes, leafy coves and snug harbors, woods and fields, and gulls circling the farmland. Here are excellent fishing grounds, the home of the Virginia oyster men, and here ducks, geese, and swans make their winter resort. A detached part of Virginia is the seventy-five-mile-long Great Peninsula, and offshore are the sand reefs and dunes of Asseateague and other lovely and uninhabited islands that beg for safekeeping. A hint of the Deep South comes with the sudden appearance of stunted, wind-driven live oaks on the south shore of Chesapeake Bay.

Beyond Norfolk, a naval base and no beauty spot, to be sure, dark shapes in the bamboo grass mark the edge of the thousand-square-mile boggy wilderness known as the Dismal Swamp. This is the Virginia of "Carry Me Back" and peanuts fame. The Roanoke area has splendid man-made lakes, but now, going westward, the Virginia landscape opens up in exhilarating splendor as the Blue Ridge Mountains rise. The highways that vein the five hundred and seventy-five miles of the Blue Ridge introduce the beauty seeker to a still tranquil and satisfying world of woods, peaks and forests, mountain meadows and wild flowers—trillium, columbine, mountain laurel, pinkster and flame azalea, catawba and rosebay rhododendron, or the Indian-festival colors of autumn. The road rises and dips southward to the Great Smokies of North Carolina and Tennessee; the sunsets can be magnificent at heights of four to five thousand feet; the mountains seem made for tough mountaineers who prefer the wilderness life to what lies below. The Blue Ridge in its unconfined, steep-sloped spread is the mecca of Southerner and Northerner alike who can't stand the woes of civilization.

Near Abingdon, the Great Valley of Virginia (the Shenandoah Valley forms a part of it) opens through the tumultuously contoured Blue Ridge, and here are found the fantastic shapes of eroded limestone in the famed caverns. Old Virginia in the west, with its split-rail fences and farmers' wives in sunbonnets, combines the simplicity of the past and the grandeur of still more ridges, rushing streams, and rhododendron-mantled forests with the moneyed flavor of the Warm Springs Inn and the Homestead at Hot Springs. The western part of Virginia may be the most beautiful part of all. There remains "Mr. Jefferson's University," the University of Virginia at Charlottesville, with its great rotunda, exquisite green quadrangle, and a formal charm that appears to unite, in one place, the attributes of a state almost overblessed with grandeur. Thomas Jefferson's own house, designed by him and in recent history tastefully restored, overlooks the university from a distant hill, and is one of the more interesting, and most visited, mansions in the country.

West Virginia

A state of gaunt and rugged beauty, and incredible greenness, with a lingering hillbilly flavor and a divided Civil War inheritance (it has long been thought of as the illegitimate child of the States) West Virginia presents an unbelievable contrast with its remote, mountainous hamlets and the carpeted lushness of the nation's premier resort, the Greenbrier at White Sulphur Springs.

Thomas Jefferson once wrote that it was worth crossing the Atlantic to see, at Harpers Ferry (only fifty-five miles from Washington, D.C.), the place where the Shenandoah River flows into the Potomac through a gap in the Blue Ridge Mountains.

The desolation of West Virginia comes almost as a shock after the neat farmlands of Pennsylvania, Virginia, and Maryland, yet its industrial towns, such as Charleston and Wheeling, have a Chicago-like drive, and in the northeast the state seems like an extension of the Old Dominion. It is a chopped-up, heterogeneous state: It is still proud of its frontier heritage (it produced the mother of Abraham Lincoln), yet can be, in parts, as silky and elegant as the best of its eastern neighbor, Virginia.

Kentucky

The institution of the state park has been mentioned here and there in this commentary, and while space prohibits discussion of the outstanding state preservations east of the Mississippi, it is certainly obligatory to single out the state-park system of Kentucky. It is a state that boasts the best parks system in America and a medley of artificial lakes for boating and fishing that are not only superbly managed but show a decent regard for conservation. Accommodations are frequently in the luxury category and often put to shame the national parks' lodgings, which are leased to private operators.

Lake Cumberland, for example—described by Michael Frome as "shaped like a coiling serpent, more than a mile wide at some points, with twisting arms and legs, and several tails"—has twelve hundred and fifty miles of shoreline and is part of the Cumberland River, which has its source in the rugged mountains of east Kentucky, winds through Appalachian coal fields and valleys, curves into Tennessee, then back into Kentucky, and finally dumps into the Ohio River near Paducah. From the park resort, cut into bluffs two hundred and fifty feet above the water, there is an almost nostalgically Swiss panorama of islands and cliffs and green hills; neither lights nor structures mar the view. Lunker walleye and big black bass fill the lake, and in May and June large-mouth bass jam the lake, along with the boats of entranced fishermen.

Kentucky has more than fifteen state resort parks to compete with Cumberland for attention, and they are uniformly attractive with modern lodges built of glass, native stone, and wood. Here, on the wooded shoreline edging a river or lake, intelligent programs of nature talks and films, guided walks, nature trails, wild flowers, bird watching, sports programs, and even square dancing can be enjoyed.

At Cumberland Falls, the "Niagara of the South" and Kentucky's pre-eminent beauty spot, one has the opportunity for a rare hike along the Cumberland River, which flows quite a way through the Daniel Boone National Forest. For about eighteen miles this is a fisherman's paradise, a wilderness river canyon replete with mudcat and gig frogs, and one can camp under cliffs surrounded by laurel and hemlock.

"Kentucky is discovering its own resources and talent through these places," the conservationist-minded Frome points out. "Old history, long forgotten, is being rediscovered, too. Boone State Park, where Daniel Boone established his fort at the end of the Wilderness Trail, is a new area awaiting development and display. In due course another lodge will rise on the site, with a picture window facing the limestone bluffs of the Kentucky River, and with a nature trail leafing through the 'great meadowland beyond the woods' that drew Boone and his people into this pioneer country."

Kentucky is as noted for its "Bluegrass country" as it is for its Louisville Derby. And at Lexington, the Bluegrass center, lies Calumet Farm, one of many exceptional breeding farms for thoroughbreds and as pretty a sight as any lover of horses could hope to see. Farther west, on the Ohio River, the borderline between Kentucky and Indiana, is the state capital, Frankfort. Louisville is a large and rambling city, from which riverboats run southwestward to Cairo and the great Mississippi.

North Carolina

"The state begins with the brightness of sea sands and ends with the loneliness of the Smokies reaching in chill and cloud to the sky. It stretches from the break of the Atlantic to the still of mountain coves, from sunlit capes to shadowed valleys five hundred miles away—from the low river-fed acres of the Coastal Plain to the rocky Piedmont and on to the hanging slopes of the Blue Ridge." Such is the thumbnail portrait of his native state by Ovid Williams Pierce, but what a varied amount of landscape it embraces! It is a soft and scenic state from edge to edge, from high in the tumbled Blue Ridge at Blowing Rock to the flat coastlands at Wilmington, where snowy egrets still fly and perch amid the lush vegetation. Its university towns, Chapel Hill and Durham, are extremely pleasant, and Charlotte and Raleigh, the major cities, are eminently livable places.

Coastal North Carolina, the Outer Banks—the rib of the continent that reaches down from Nags Head to capes Hatteras, Lookout, and Fear—was closed off for more than two hundred years, but today most of it is accessible and not all of it strikes the heart with its beauty. At commercial Nags Head the high dune is best seen from the tiny breakers on the empty beaches, and Kitty Hawk, reconstructed to simulate conditions under which the Wright Brothers first took to the air, gamely fights the nostalgia-versus-commercialism battle. Most of the Outer Banks, luckily, is now a national seashore, and south of Nags Head the empty stretches of sand still provide a primitive atmosphere. And all the way down to Hatteras, one can climb a dune and stake out miles of beach in blissful privacy.

Roanoke Island is the well-known setting, with the smell of red honeysuckle and partridge-berry blossoms filling the air, of Paul Green's *The Lost Colony;* and despite the passage of years, it still has the power to move audiences to wonder at the disappearance of the early colonists into the wilderness. Blackbeard's ghost, romantics say, still haunts Ocrakoke Island, where wild ponies once ran free. From Oregon Inlet to Ocrakoke the sea, sand, and beach grass in their unspoiled state provide a lonely, contemplative setting.

The Great Dismal Swamp, at the upper edge of North Carolina's coast plain and spilling over into Virginia, is still largely inaccessible. A spongy quagmire of cypress, black gum, and juniper that filter out the sunlight, it is truly the "region of unearthly darkness lying across sunlit land" that Pierce describes, one of the still secret places of the American terrain. But it is western North Carolina—across the Piedmont and in the powerful presence of the ragged escarpment of the Blue Ridge—that really captures one.

From Virginia the mountain chain continues past Asheville to the Smokies below, range upon beautiful range, canyons and valleys opening unexpectedly from the viewpoint of the superb Blue Ridge Parkway, lakes glittering in sunstruck valleys, still more laurel and rhododendron blanketing the forested ridges, and mountain people, natural musicians and artisans, still practicing the old skills off the beaten path. This is the country of the dulcimer and the minstrel, lonesome-sad country, where the views are unbearably glamorous yet the people dress in homespun and make music, a recent observer reports, that seems more like a fragment of seventeenth-century England than North Carolina in the seventies. You don't really know America until you have been there.

Tennessee

The mountain country of North Carolina spills over naturally, and without sharp distinction, into Tennessee, where the Great Smoky Mountains, straddling both states, loom as the "massive high citadel of the Appalachian system."

For sheer geography and beauty, there is little that lies east of the Mississippi to rival the Great Smokies (so called because of the high haze over the tallest peaks), a truly majestic range with sixteen peaks topping six thousand feet. Most of the range is within the boundaries of the more than five hundred thousand acres of the Great Smoky Mountains National Park.

Where once a hardy, self-sufficient people plucked a rude living from the soil, isolated in their almost primitive farmhouses, today this colossal landscape (superlatives seem to come naturally to the Smokies) offers a cornucopia of gifts to the lover of simple nature: to the hiker, flower stalker, horseback rider, wanderer, camper, gypsy. View collectors can get their fill, and perhaps overabundance, from the scary winding roads and overlooks; thrill seekers can chance getting an arm bitten off by feeding the bears; tourist haters can bury themselves deep in the forests, undisturbed, undetected; lovers of pioneer history can marvel at the self-sufficient items of clothing, furniture, and utensils on display in the museums; collectors of Indian lore can find in the Cherokee Reservation interesting artifacts of a gentle, civilized tribe that the white man never did right by. Hundreds of miles of streams are stocked with bass and trout for the fisherman; in June the hills are a mass of pink azaleas; six hundred miles of horse and

31

foot trails wind throughout the park. From the top of Clingmans Dome (6642 feet) on a clear day, one looks down on a sea of clouds shrouding the peaks below—perhaps the most stunning view of all in this preserve molded by nature and preserved for man.

Memphis is one of the Mississippi's pre-eminent river towns, the town of King Cotton and one of the early birthplaces of American jazz, and for the most part, a courtly place where life is slow and leisurely and where many Old South customs are rigorously cherished.

Nashville, a business-minded city, still holds on to its strong cultural traditions, and Chattanooga, despite its drabness, is located in a gorgeous setting of mountains, forests, and river, with the famous Lookout Mountain as its tourist magnet. Tennessee is also the home of an original and potent product, sour mash whiskey, a drink more and more Europeans are discovering, to the astonishment of their palates.

South Carolina Georgia

Another kind of Southern nature—lush, junglelike, spooky—is found along the coasts of South Carolina and Georgia. This is the Gullah country, ghostly and unique, flat and fertile and sensuous. Maggie Davis describes it in the following way.

"Seen from the air, the coast looks smooth and black-green, with a chain of islands lying seaward. From Waccamaw Island above Charleston, South Carolina, to Cumberland Island in Georgia, just above the Florida line, the plains and marshlands of the low-country South spread out, well irrigated by the wide, brown rivers with names like Altamaha and Pee Dee. On the Atlantic, the island beaches appear snowy with sand as fine and white as drifted confectioners' sugar.

"There's always an aura of gentle rot on the Gullah coast. The natives usually refer to it as 'just the old wind from the papuh mill, honey.' But unfortunately for visitors, this is not entirely true. When it comes to nostalgia, the Gullah country has, in addition to the kraft industry, a stink of sea tides and cape jessamine, burning pine and honeysuckle and many other things, mixed, occasionally, with the aroma of maturing fish bait. Once you get used to them—the stink and the elusive mysteries, the dazzling white beaches and dim back roads arched over with moss-hung trees—the Gullah coast is, as travelers invariably remark, 'like no other place on earth.'"

Gullah country charm can be sinister, even at ultrawealthy Hilton Head. One constantly senses that humid, "whispering blackness with the incessant wash of river tides on empty sands," and the Gullah people themselves, striking ebony blacks descended from slaves imported from West Africa, are notoriously reticent. It is dank, haunted country, where one still feels palably the presence of ghosts.

A far cry from the Gullah country is amenable, elaborately civilized Charleston. This delectable city of garden walls and stately houses on the famed Battery overlooking the Atlantic is one whose charm in springtime cannot be resisted, even by those who try. "All cities are engaging (in spring)," Frances Gray Patton drily says, "but Charleston has had the chance to practice for spring all winter." Its showy plantation gardens —Cypress, Magnolia, and Middleton—"foam with color," and its cypress groves and live oaks and banks of azaleas, footpaths and rustic bridges, lagoons and canals, lawns and terraces, leave one rapturously impressed. Charleston is a city to explore on foot, a city of wisteria and self-conscious Catfish Row and chimney pots and steeples and loving restorations, all "civilized grace" to a fare-thee-well. And those who admire it most, unsentimentally, feel it is the prettiest little city in the world. And perhaps it is.

Another aspect of the Deep South—the South of backwoods quaintness that gets a popular comic-strip acceptance in characters like Pogo—is the Okefenokee Swamp in southeastern Georgia, the seven hundred square miles of freshwater swampland that edge over into Florida.

32

The Seminoles once called this area of sepia lakes, moss-hung cypress, and mysterious streams the "land of trembling earth." Vast marshes, called "prairies," fill its sixty thousand acres, and the National Wildlife Refuge that embraces four-fifths of the gigantic swamp harbors an extraordinary variety of life, including bear, deer, bobcats, alligators, and many aquatic birds. To lovers of this odd corner of America, the label "the most beautiful and fantastic landscape in the world" comes easy. Rare plants have been pulled from the swamp floor, and miles of cypress stand in dense formations; if you stamp on this "trembling earth," the trees will shake. Sandhill cranes and round-tailed muskrats are found here in abundance, and the swamp vegetation is interesting —for example, the gardenia, with white-and-yellow blooms that are a pleasing slash of color against the dark green vegetation from May to October.

In the spring the watery vegetation also yields such blooms as white and yellow water lilies, pickerelweed, swamp marigold, and iris. The Okefenokee deserves to be called "a unique and beautiful natural wonderland in America."

Georgia's two urban centers are as apart in mood as they are in miles. Atlanta, entirely rebuilt since it was razed in the Civil War and almost rebuilt a second time, is among America's most modern cities. Sparkling Savannah, at the top of the Peach Tree State's short sea line, still has its old sections, older ways, and a Southern seaport ambiance that lures many visitors to venture south from Charleston to take a look. It is a city to be lived in, a city of twenty exquisite historic parks and squares; of famed Factor's Walk, where the cotton brokers worked, with buildings connected to the street by footbridges; of bursting markets and a leisurely river-front section; and of cobbled streets and beautifully crafted houses varying in style from Regency to Victorian Gothic.

Florida

Of the overdeveloped and wracked state of Florida—the southernmost on the Atlantic seaboard, noted equally for its fruit industry, its white sands and year-round sun and fun resorts on both the Atlantic and Gulf shores, its retirement communities, and its historic St. Augustine—only the Everglades would appear to survive as a reservoir of primitive nature in the raw.

But even around the Everglades, intrusions of commerce are causing profound concern for its future as a place for human enjoyment. Yet what survives in this steaming world where life has spawned for millions of years is indeed wondrous. *Pa-hay-okee* in Indian language means "grassy water," which is what the Everglades are: a river of grass. "But their grass is not grass as we know it," writes Benedict Thielen, whose appreciation of the Everglades is that of a lyrical naturalist. "It does not bend and ripple under the wind. It stands stiff, straight, and unyielding. It is really not grass at all but a flowering sedge, one of the oldest forms of green life on earth. It grows with fierce luxuriance, eight, ten, and in some places, fifteen feet high. It is set with tiny, sharp teeth of silica, and this is why they call it saw grass. The blades of this grass are truly blades—they can tear off a man's clothes and rip open his flesh. Like an impenetrable stockade they stand here, upthrust in their countless millions, a wilderness of sharpened swords. Spreading over thirty-five hundred square miles, the saw grass grows in the shallow water, fed by the sun and the deep rich rot of forty centuries of alternating life and death. . . . The grass does not move. But below it, invisibly, the water moves . . . from Lake Okeechobee southward, it flows slowly to the sea."

Sloughs and swamps. Clumps of mangroves whose tannin in the roots stains the water a deep brown only to turn blue under a blue sky. Cypress swamps. Chalky-blue and lime-green shallows. Ridges of limestone. Ponds and water holes and lakes. Trees smitten dead by hurricanes. Everywhere a shining wetness and heat. It is an Amazonian scene, lonely and mysterious. Thielen describes its luxuriating life:

"In this heat and wetness life breeds and spawns as it has for millions of years. Mostly, it is shy, night-feeding, night-hunting, but you sense its presence and feel that eyes are watching you: the green-glowing eyes of panthers, the liquid eyes of deer, the cold eyes of rattlesnakes and cotton-mouths, the black-masked eyes of raccoons. These last you will probably see as they move across the road with their high-shouldered, flat-footed shuffle, or as with their deft little hands they wash their food in a patch of clear water among the mangroves. A slow swirl in one of the coastal rivers may show where a manatee—fat, wrinkled, childishly blue-eyed—is feeding on water weeds. The clawed top of a palmetto may show where a bear has climbed to eat its tender heart.

"As the awakening day creeps, then suddenly explodes over the rim of the sea, the air is filled with bird cries, bird song, and the beating of wings. They rise in clouds from the shores of Bear Lake, or Whitewater Bay, or Lostman's River. In summer dawns a hundred thousand rise from Duck Rock alone. The sky is written over with the patterns of their flight—the upward spiraling of white pelicans, the hurried water-skimming of cormorants and ducks, the wing-folded dive of ospreys, hawks, and eagles, the scissoring clip of the frigate birds, the slow flap of the ibis, herons, and egrets."

In this red-mangrove jungle, this rich and heavy dampness, the feeling is of being in a riotous greenhouse. Orchids and air plants, ferns and mosses, palmetto and mahogany and gumbo limbo thrive and multiply. Unseen life stirs in the warm ooze. Helicon butterflies drift through the still junglelike branches, crabs scuttle, and at times there is almost unbearable stillness, a silence. An alligator plops in the muck while a sandhill hopper crane preens herself nearby. Parts of the Everglades yield human bones, Indian mounds, deadly vegetation such as the poisonwood and red-mottled manchineel, and nasty snakes—the pygmy rattler, for example. Parts of it are tame, too, but it is those rank and Amazonian places that give to the Everglades the excitement of having stumbled into an unearthly strangeness.

The Florida Keys—another part of the state that its permissive laxity cannot entirely ruin—was called by the Spaniards in the sixteenth century *Los Martires* because of the islands' twisted shapes. The narrow chain embraces almost nine hundred islands, a one-hundred-and-twenty-mile link extending thirty air miles from Miami to Key West, a mere seventy miles north of the Tropic of Cancer. John D. MacDonald, the well-known mystery writer who is immensely knowledgeable about the Keys, analyzes their special flavor:

"The strange way nature created this string of islands rules out any chance of a water table. The upper keys rest upon the bony skeleton of an ancient coral reef. The lower keys are formed of egg-shaped particles of limestone cemented together to form a kind of rock called Miami oolite. But both halves are above water only because of the staggering and unbelievable life-persistence of an almost microscopic little marine creature called Foraminifera that has deposited two miles of limestone atop a narrow formation that happened to be the submerged foothills of the Appalachian Mountains.

"Foraminifera left no chance of fresh water, but it certainly made the great flats and shallows of the Atlantic shore on the south side of the Keys and the Florida Bay shore on the north uncommonly lovely. With no silt to wash into the seas—there are no rivers—the waters are as crystalline as Bahamian waters that reflect, amid an almost excessive profusion of shades of blue ranging from baby pastel to indigo and over into lavender and purple, the tawny sandbars, dark blotches of bottom weed, white reflections of limestone outcroppings. Boatmen 'read' the water by color, and run their shallow-draft fishing skiffs through unmarked, ever-changing channels with almost insolent skill."

The Keys are delightfully named, especially the off-keys that cars can't reach from the overcrowded Overseas Highway that links the main keys. Waltz, Snipe, Old Dan Mangrove, Big Harper, Hard Up, Little Swash, Top Tree Hammock, Little Knock-medown—a fey imagination has been at work in this southeastern tip of America. The Keys, claims MacDonald, "offer pleasures unique in our world and our times," and the best way to enjoy them is, of course, by boat. "The spring weeks before the rains begin and the weeks before Christmas, after the hurricane season ends, are the most delightful times, and a month is not too little to allow for poking around. There are not many places left in the world where you can dinghy across the shallows to a distant white line of beach and find no physical reason to doubt that you are the first person ever to walk on that beach.

"And most of this special away-from-the-road world is available to those who trail a small boat down to one of the places along the Keys, where they can live in a tent and have the long bright days on the water, the fishing and exploring, shelling and swimming."

Mr. MacDonald, in his enthusiasm, could easily start a new stampede to the Florida Keys, a paradise for fishermen and yachtsmen and swimmers, and for people who love to be out in the sun without the backdrop of a noisy Miami or the entertainments of well-groomed Palm Beach or the Easter student invasion at Fort Lauderdale.

Not that the expensive resort areas of Florida are all to be avoided: Palm Beach is beautiful as well as snobbish, and Boca Raton and Delray are amenable; and on the west cost Sarasota and its keys are thriving with assorted nature and shore lovers. The great virtue of Florida is its variety, from its quiet capital, Tallahassee, in the north, through its enormous citrus belt and lakes in the center to the Cuban flavor of Tampa on the west coast. It is both America's playground and a valuable agricultural asset, a state of many attractive and often conflicting opposites.

Louisiana

In the Deep South is Louisiana, with its strongly French patina—a state that boasts the sumptuous gustatory pleasures of historic New Orleans, located at the mouth of the great Mississippi River, and the remnants of a vanished French culture. Unlike South Carolina's Charleston, New Orleans does not have the sense of loving and fastidious preservation, except in the picturesque *Vieux Carré*, one of the oldest and most photographed urban quarters anywhere in the country. Some say New Orleans is more a place to eat in than to visit (in the Bourbon Street district the pick of restaurants bewilders) and certainly its crawfish, shrimp creole, and gumbos are generally excellent and fortifying.

The grand plantations on the river road that leads from New Orleans toward Baton Rouge are classically handsome in settings of tropical vegetation and lushness. After the brick and ironwork architectural treasures of the *Vieux Carré* perhaps the most photographed antiquity of the Deep South is Oak Alley, built in 1836 beside the Mississippi near Vacherie. This spectacular estate boasts two geometrically straight rows of giant oaks that form a quarter-mile-long arch over the driveway leading up to the white-columned house. The architecture of the mansion is both grand and simple: two levels of wide porches encircle it, and the richly furnished rooms, crystal chandeliers, broad staircase, great central hall, and beautiful formal gardens inspire the requisite nostalgia for an unreal past.

By contrast, Louisana's bayou country, the so-called Evangeline country, remains sturdy and enduring. A workable and still-valid description of it was given years ago by Hamilton Basso:

"The bayou system of lower Louisiana is best likened to a watery cobweb. Some of the bayous that make up the lines of the web are relatively large, well-mapped waterways—Bayou Teche, Bayou Lafourche, and Bayou Terrebonne being the three most notable—while others are small uncharted streams known only to the few families that live among their banks. The swamps into which many of the bayous find their way have a special eerie moss-draped beauty, and there is no place in America where one sees a greater variety of birds, but the chances are that this kind of beauty is an acquired taste. For along with the birds—the cranes and herons, the ducks and geese, the cardinals and hummingbirds—there is the finest collection of snakes this side of the tropics. Then, too, the somber stretches of swamp, in which the best of trappers sometimes lose their way, are hung with a profound, almost palpable silence that seems to have gone unbroken since the start of time."

Avery Island, a few miles southwest of New Iberia (which boasts the lovely plantation "The Shadows"), offers one of the great bird sanctuaries as well as exceptionally fine gardens. Fluttering through the thick foliage is the largest colony of egrets in the United States as well as blue herons, mockingbirds, wrens, and summer tanagers. The flora: groves of giant bamboo, arches of wisteria, fields of iris and camellias and chrysanthemums, Indian soap trees, Egyptian papyrus, Chinese banana trees, Brazilian rubber plants; as well as such hardy American natives as oak, redbud, magnolia, and dogwood. Avery Island was once described by James A. Maxwell as "an astonishing circle of land two miles in diameter which rises like an improbable bubble from the surrounding marsh." It is a modest-size plot with an engaging freshness.

Mississippi

Southern writers have always been a breed apart, and why the South historically and continuously has spurted forth such a fountain of literary talent is a question perhaps best left to the scholars. One fact does constantly emerge in the reading of "place" writing on the South by Southerners and that is their profound, subjective, almost mystical feeling for the Southern landscape. Westerners write movingly about their big open spaces and New Englanders love their land, although appalled by its harshness, but Southerners *feel*, intensely—to their very marrow—about the soil from which they have sprung.

No writer has more loved (and more hated) his native state than William Faulkner, whose lifelong obsession with Mississippi took the form of novels whose literary permanence is assured and who affected two generations of America with his tragic view of his native corner. "He was born of it and his bones will sleep in it; loving it even while hating some of it. . . ." So wrote Faulkner in perhaps the only magazine article (*Holiday*, April, 1954) he ever wrote about Mississippi. The article is both autobiography and an adumbration of the themes that dominated his novels; a long threnody about Mississippi, past and present, that includes personal anecdotes, the state's bloodied history, the planter aristocracy, the invading Snopeses, the harassed yet enduring blacks, the mood and rhythm and changing contours of the landscape. One section grips the imagination with its sustained power. It deals with the wrecking force of the country's grandest river, the "Old Man," the Mississippi, a torrent gone crazy in spring, and the urgent human battle to fight or be swept away:

"The Old Man: all his little contributing streams levee'd too, along with him, and paying none of the dykes any heed at all when it suited his mood and fancy, gathering water all the way from Montana to Pennsylvania every generation or so and rolling it down the artificial gut of his victims' puny and baseless hoping, piling the water up, not fast, just inexorably, giving plenty of time to measure his crest and telegraph ahead, even warning of the exact day almost when he would enter the house and float the piano out of it and the pictures off the walls, and even remove the house itself if it were not securely fastened down.

"Inexorable and unhurried, overpassing one by one his little confluent feeders and shoving the water into them until for days their current would flow backward, upstream: as far upstream as Wylie's Crossing above Jefferson. The little rivers were dyked, too, but back here was the land of individualists: remnants and descendants of the tall men now taken to farming, and of Snopeses who were more than individualists: they were Snopeses, so that where the owners of the thousand-acre plantations along the Big River confederated as one man with sandbags and machines and their Negro tenants and wage-hands to hold the sandboils and the cracks, back here the owner of the hundred- or two-hundred-acre farm patrolled his section of levee with a sandbag in one hand and his shotgun in the other, lest his upstream neighbor dynamite it to save his (the upstream neighbor's) own.

"Piling up the water while white man and Negro worked side by side in shifts in the mud and the rain, with automobile headlights and gasoline flares and kegs of whisky and coffee boiling in fifty-gallon batches in scoured and scalded oil drums; lapping, tentative, almost innocently, merely inexorable (no hurry, his) among and beneath and between and finally over the frantic sandbags, as if his whole purpose had been merely to give man another chance to prove, not to him but to man, just how much the human body could bear, stand, endure; then, having let man prove it, doing what he could have done at any time these past weeks if so minded: removing with no haste, nor any particular malice or fury either, a mile or two miles of levee and coffee drums and whisky kegs and gas flares in one sloughing collapse, gleaming dully for a little while yet among the parallel cotton middles until the fields vanished along with the roads and lanes and at last the towns themselves.

"Vanished, gone beneath one vast yellow motionless expanse, out of which projected only the tops of trees and telephone poles and the decapitations of human dwelling-places like enigmatic objects placed by inscrutable and impenetrable design on a dirty mirror; and the mounds of the predecessors on which, among a tangle of moccasins, bear and horses and deer and mules and wild turkeys and cows and domestic chickens waited patient in mutual armistice; and the levees themselves, where among a jumble of uxorious flotsam the young continued to be born and the old to die, not from exposure but from simple and normal time and decay, as if man and his destiny were in the end stronger even than the river which had dispossessed him, inviolable by and invincible to alteration.

"Then, having proved that too, he—the Old Man—would withdraw, not retreat, subside, back from the land slowly and inexorably too, emptying the confluent rivers and bayous back into the old vain hopeful gut, but so slowly and gradually that not the waters seemed to fall but the flat earth itself to rise, creep in one plane back into light and air again: one constant stain of yellow-brown at one constant altitude on telephone poles and the walls of gins and houses and stores as though the line had been laid off with a transit and painted in one gigantic unbroken brush stroke, the earth itself one alluvial inch higher, the rich dirt one inch deeper, drying into long cracks beneath the hot fierce glare of May: but not for long, because almost at once came the plow, the plowing and planting already two months late but that did not matter: the cotton man-tall once more by August and whiter and denser still by picking time, as if the Old Man said, 'I do what I want to, when I want to. But I pay my way.'

"And the boats, of course, they projected above that yellow and liquid plane and even moved upon it: the skiffs and scows of fishermen and trappers, the launches of the United States Engineers who operated the Levee Commission, and one small shallow-draught steamboat steaming in paradox among and across the cotton fields themselves, its pilot not a riverman but a farmer who knew where the submerged fences were, its masthead lookout a mechanic with a pair of pliers to cut the telephone wires to pass the smokestack through: no paradox really, since on the River it had resembled a house to begin with, so that here it looked no different from the baseless houses it steamed among and on occasion even strained at top boiler pressure to overtake, like a mallard drake after a fleeing mallard hen.

"But these boats were not enough, very quickly not near enough, the Old Man meant business indeed this time. So now there began to arrive from the Gulf ports the shrimp trawlers and pleasure cruisers and Coast Guard cutters whose bottoms had known only salt water and the mouths of tidal rivers, to be run still by their salt-water crews but conned by the men who knew where the submerged roads and fences were for the good reason that they had been running mule-plow furrows along them or up to them all their lives; sailing among the swollen carcasses of horses and mules and deer and cows and sheep to pluck the Old Man's patient flotsam, black and white, out of trees and the roofs of gins and cotton sheds and floating cabins and the second-story windows of houses and office buildings; then—the salt-water men, to whom land was either a featureless treeless salt marsh or a snake- and alligator-infested swamp impenetrable with trumpet vine and Spanish moss, some of whom had never even seen the earth into which were driven the spiles supporting the houses they lived in—staying on even after they were no longer needed, as though waiting to see emerge from the water what sort of country it was which bore the economy on which the people—men and women, black and white, more of black than white even, ten to one more—lived whom they had saved; seeing the land for that moment before mule and plow altered it right up to the water's receding edge, then back into the River again before the trawlers and cruisers and cutters became marooned into canted and useless rubble too along with the ruined hencoops and cowsheds and privies; back onto the Old Man, shrunken once more into his normal banks, drowsing and even innocent looking, as if it were something else besides him that had changed, for a little time anyway, the whole face of the adjacent earth."

Alabama

A state more known for its courthouse politics and bad press and Black Belt meanness than the endowments it should be proud of: the pretty lakes and hills in the red-clay country of the north, the roaring productive capacity of Birmingham, often known as the "Pittsburgh of the South," the dazzling gardens of Montgomery and Mobile that often rival those of Charleston in their lavish blooms, the seafront activity of Mobile, the handsome Greek Revival plantation houses, the soft culture (music and good books and distinguished food) that its quiet, retiring, civilized upper-middle class enjoys.

This is a state that for too long lived in the glory of its pre-Civil War past—when every plantation owner knew his Latin and Greek—and now hopes there is a promise in a go-getting future, spearheaded by its bright businessmen, who shun the philosophy of the back-country towns in favor of the more productive virtues of the classical Deep South.

SOUTH
BY SOUTHWEST

Not part of the South, nor indigenously Midwest, Southwest, or West are the states of Arkansas and Oklahoma, bordered on the east by Mississippi, on the south by Texas, and on the north by Kansas and Missouri.

Arkansas

The former joke state because of its backwardness, Arkansas is like many states a divided being—in the east a rich, but for the most part rather dull, flatland that is excellent farming country (a farmer can plow a furrow a straight mile long and think nothing of it); in the west hilly, Indian-oriented in its past, and embracing a large chunk of the Ozarks that, as in Missouri, still throw up the old ways of mountain men, of mountain music, and the mores of hill people whom primitive painters still love to record.

In the center of the state, on the banks of the Arkansas River, lies Little Rock, its capital and biggest city. To the west, toward Oklahoma, are woodlands, lakes, and mountain streams, the natural features of western Arkansas. And in places like Eureka Springs a quaint throwback to Elizabethan days can still be felt in the Arkansan's love of musical festivals, singing, and stomping. That, combined with its wilderness areas, gives this region of Arkansas—an area of high lonesome ridges and valleys—a sense of rustic remoteness in time from most of America that is fascinating.

Oklahoma

Like Kansas, Oklahoma is a state of old bleeding grounds, of nasty engagements against the plains Indians—Osage, Cherokee, Kiowa, Choctaw, Pawnee—and of lawless gunslingers, badmen, and feisty oil prospectors. Rich plains, oil lands, ranchlands, timbered mountains, lakes, and rivers: It is a Confederate state historically that is spiritually allied with the West. Its two big cities are Oklahoma City, the capital, at the very heart of the state, and Tulsa lying northeast of it, below the Osage Indian Reservation.

This is Will Rogers' state, homespun America in humor and style, as well as a state of moving Indian heritage, the state of the Cherokee nation and of John Steinbeck's Okies who uprooted themselves from the dusty emptiness and made their dismal trek to California. Oklahoma is a state of the rage for wealth and the eponym for the best in musical nostalgia; but most of all, a state of the oil derrick and of romantic memories of the time it was a free-for-all territory and the white man and the Indian played out their duels to the death.

THE AMERICAN MIDDLE GROUND

Many Americans think of the Middle West as a vast, bleak land to be hurried through as quickly as possible on the way west or eastward toward the tidy quality of New England. It is both the granary of America and an industrial sprawl—much of it ugly and disheartening—that fights against the fruitful abundance of the land itself.

Ohio, Indiana, Illinois, Iowa—this is the Middle West that unrolls from, say, Pittsburgh to the western banks of the Missouri River. A Midwest of punishing summer heat and frigid winter cold, of blissful short-lived springs, and dazzling, flaming, hushed autumns. It is the heartland, the bounty place, cornfields and prairies, small woods, big rivers, large cities and neat towns, lush farms, rural affluence. It is the arena of hard work, conservative instincts, the pitting of man against nature, an immense "squaredom" (in the popular mind) with an occasional outburst of artistic and cultural creativity, especially in the excellent state universities; of prosperity and dullness, towns that still bear out every complaint voiced by the frustrated characters in *Winesburg, Ohio*, Sherwood Anderson's withering account of small-town life in Ohio. Well, perhaps.

It is curious that the Midwesterners from Ohio to Iowa would perhaps not choose to live anywhere else (except upon retirement, and then Florida or California), and they love their land with an agreeable passion. They should: they have made it extraordinarily fertile.

There is a second Midwest, the upper tier—Michigan, Wisconsin, and Minnesota—that has an altogether different shape and that exudes an aromatic flavor associated with blue skies, deep woods and forests, thousands of blue lakes, fresh air, boating and hunting and fishing, the right to seclusion and loneliness: North Woods and the Deep North, the legendary land of Paul Bunyan and lumbermen's tales and Indian trappers, French explorers, Scandinavian energy, the land of milk and cheese and rolling farmlands.

Outside of the industrial cities, this is a sportsman's and wanderer's land, a land to get lost in, dream in; a land where you can enter into a compact of personal magic with nature. Natives who stay away too long from the North Country are besieged by an unbearable nostalgia. One remembers the young Hemingway, musing in his Left Bank garret and strolling along the boulevards of Paris, recalling—and later fictionalizing—his youthful days *Up in Michigan*, and the intense pleasure that the combination of fishing, primitive nature, and solitude can bring to the exposed loner. The beauty part is that pockets of solitary splendor still exist in the North Country, and the best descriptions have been made by native writers who have an almost physical relationship with the landscape.

Start with the Ohio River, on the eastern flank of the Midwest, which slowly gathers speed until it rushes headlong to meet the Old Man at Cairo (pronounced CARE-oh), Illinois. The river connotes many levels of life to novelist Davis Grubb, who grew up in Moundsville, West Virginia, and who writes about the valley of the Ohio with felt passion but without a trace of sentimentality. One level is the nostalgia people feel for the vanished "sugared, lacy stacks of the great steamboats."

"Some sentimental cynics grieve for the halcyon days of the great river epoch;

they say the time of the riverboat is gone. Yet nothing is, in fact, really gone but a packet of useless legends. Gone the calliope which announced spring among the wake-robin tree shadows of my boyhood, long before jonquil or crocus came, long before green frogs praised winter's death among the cattails at Grave Creek's mouth, before the twelfth-generation family of wrens returned to their miniature, ancestral home in our rose arbor; before buttercup or bird's-foot violet embroidered the sweet name of April into the sampler fabric of that blessed earth. Gone, too, the whistles of the old steamboats: three, four and six-toned chords like the reedy, throaty pipes of baroque organs."

River people are special, too, and one frequently wonders what demonic force ties them to the ebb and flow of the water that too often only succeeds in destroying them.

"Why do riverfolk stay?" writes Grubb. "Why do they come back? The temptation is to give the question that romantic answer which is difficult to believe. Which is unfortunate because the romantic answer is the only one. Riverfolk love the river. Sometimes they hate the river but sometimes a woman hates her man, too, and men beat girls for whom they would die. So riverfolk love the river and sometimes they hate the river and once they have forgiven the river they are all the more hopelessly enamored. The river cannot drive them away. They must come back. Industry and progress must move them. But the river cannot make them budge a foot. Some never move from their shacks because they are poor. But more than the poor are the lovers—who cherish the river and hate the river and forgive the river and come back after forgiveness to love her all the more."

It is a statement that could easily apply to all the great rivers of America, and to those attached to them with a passion that seems, to the outsider, just this side of madness.

Of the great Midwestern outdoor pastimes, none holds the fancy of the multitudes more than fishing—quiet, easy, lazy, contemplative fishing. And the fish that apparently holds the imagination along the Ohio are, in Grubb's words, "the black catfish moving along the river floor in their prehistoric and beautiful ugliness. . . . Rivermen love him—with gingerly respect and cautious fingers. He is tough to tempt to a trotline hook because he is a bottom dweller and, in general, since his food drifts down to him, he seldoms rises. A chunk of laundry soap is the best bait, says one school. Another swears by little pellets of river mud mixed with the crumbled flesh of creek minnows. Every fisherman from Pittsburgh to Cairo claims his bait is best. No one has thought to ask the catfish. Read his homely face and perhaps you may know the answer. His mouth is wide with lips which smile, bemused; he has no teeth but his maw is lined with a ragged, bony plate with which, it is said, he can shred a careless fisherman's arm from elbow to finger. His brow is set with rubbery, long black horns. These tentacles can inflict painful, festering puncture wounds in hands that don't know the slick, proper way of skinning them. The question of catfish age and size is an area of discussion which ranges between the preposterous and the impossible."

The only omission in Davis Grubb's superb description is the gustatory: what fish fry in these parts is complete without a mess of catfish?

Ohio

This unquestionably is the All-American State: raging industry balanced by pretty, white New England-type towns; faultlessly maintained farms played off against grim and ugly modern cities. "Ohio is neither East nor West or South," writes a native son, Bentz Plagemann. "It just sits where it is, and never shouts to make itself heard—it just speaks in its calm, flat, unregional, unaccented, uninflected voice. The bounty of Lake Erie presses down on the top of Ohio, and the state bends with its weight, and at the bottom the river flows, the Beautiful Ohio, where the moonlight glows, where the barges float by, carrying the hard-earned wealth down to the great Mississippi. Ohio stands straight between its straight borders, plain and full of common sense."

In Northern Ohio, across the Vermilion River and east to Pennsylvania and south to just below Akron, lies one of the most attractive sections of the Middle West, the Western Reserve. This is "the architect's and amateur historian's paradise," claims Plagemann, "a region of America waiting to be discovered by the traveler." The names of the towns are Norwalk and North Fairfield and New London; the area is known as the "Firelands," land given to settlers from Connecticut whose homes were burned by the British during the Revolution. "Good dairy land, where the Classical Revival farmhouses bear the signature of their architects in such unusual details as recessed second-story porches, and fretwork on porticos and pilasters; outlined at night against the setting sun on land flat as the Texas Panhandle, lonely and austere, waiting for a Marquand to record their almost forgotten tales."

Much of northern Ohio appears in passing to be more New England than New England itself, with elm-shaded commons and Greek Revival houses and hidden villages on back roads. One has only to travel northeast beyond vigorous Cleveland to see this still-green and pleasant world.

Ohio also shows off to good advantage the Pickaway Plains south of Columbus, where the Scioto flows between willow-shaded banks, handsome farm country once bloodied by struggles between the whites and the Shawnee. South of the Pickaway Plains is Chillicothe on the Scioto River. And further south on the Ohio River emerges another New England surprise: Marietta, an orderly, pretty town, with venerable trees and gabled, stately homes—a village plucked straight out of the Berkshires and plunked down in the wilderness. Ohio has many surprises. It may be that it is not really the Middle West; the Middle West *begins* here.

Indiana

The Hoosier State, the Wabash—the twin clichés. Actually, there is a northern and southern Indiana, which Indianapolis, the capital, evenly divides. The northern Indiana is the roaring smokestacks of Gary on Lake Michigan, and South Bend some forty miles east; it is the gold dome of Notre Dame, the "great wastes and singing sands" of the famous Indiana dunes, sweet lakes with names like Wawasee, Maxinkuckee, Shipshewana, and hogs and corn, the twin deities of northern Indiana, indeed of the whole state.

Southern Indiana is a sharp contrast with the north; hilly land, full of scenery and tradition. Below, immediately across the Ohio River from Evansville is the west, and from Switzerland County in the east lies Kentucky, big and almost overpowering to the southern Hoosiers.

In Brown County, western pioneer life at its most poignant and stirring was once played out, and the state of Indiana preserves a good bit of the country in its remarkable park system. Only a native like William E. Wilson can evoke the sharp ache of this old land and an (almost) vanished life:

"The countryside here is at its best in the fall, when the foliage is aflame with color and the melancholy haze of Indiana autumn blankets the hills. Persimmons lie rotting on the ground then, and walnuts are scattered through the woods for squirrels to gather and small boys to stain their hands with. Wagons loaded with golden pumpkins creak along the steep roads, and in the fields khaki-colored fodder stands in regimented shocks. . . . Sounds come softly but with sharp clarity across the hills at this time of the year, like words whispered in the night, and the air is perfumed with hickory smoke threading skyward from the chimneys of log cabins tucked in a hundred hollows."

These words were written less than two decades ago, but already they have the melancholy ring of a lost time.

Thirteen years ago, the distinguished novelist Saul Bellow took a journey through his home state and wrote a report on his travels. It may come as a surprise to learn that Bellow, the creator of memorable urban characters whose neurotic edge-of-the-cliff adventures are the stuff of rich black humor, can also write with eloquence and passion of the external, physical world—and about the prairies of Illinois.

"Miles and miles of prairie, slowly rising and falling, sometimes give you a sense that something is in the process of becoming, or that the liberation of a great force is imminent, some power, like Michelangelo's slave only half released from the block of stone. Conceivably the mound-building Indians believed their resurrection would coincide with some such liberation, and built their graves in imitation of the low moraines deposited by the departing glaciers. But they have not yet been released and remain drowned in their waves of earth. They have left their bones, their flints and pots, their place names and tribal names and little besides except a stain, seldom vivid, on the consciousness of their white successors.

"The soil of the Illinois prairies is fat, rich and thick. After spring plowing it looks oil-blackened or colored by the soft coal which occurs in great veins throughout the state. In the fields you frequently see a small tipple, or a crazy-looking device that pumps oil and nods like the neck of a horse at a quick walk. Isolated among the cornstalks or the soybeans, the iron machine clanks and nods, stationary. Along the roads, with intervals between them as neat and even as buttons on the cuff, sit steel storage bins, in form like the tents of Mongolia. They are filled with grain. And the elevators and tanks, trucks and machines that crawl over the fields and blunder over the highways —whatever you see is productive. It creates wealth, it stores wealth, it is wealth."

On the towns of Illinois, he writes, "Galena is an old, cracked, mossy place, and looks a little crazy. An invisible giant tent caterpillar has built over it, and the sun comes through the trees as through frayed curtains. . . . There are many towns in Illinois that have been . . . bypassed, towns like Cairo and Shawneetown in the south. They flourished until the railroads made the steamboats obsolete and now they sit, the fortresses of faithful old daughters and age-broken sons who do not go away."

"The Mormons have been coming back to Nauvoo. They have opened some of the old brick and stone houses in the lower town, near the Mississippi; they have trimmed the lawns and cleaned the windows, and set out historical markers and opened views on the river which here, as it approaches Keokuk Dam, broadens and thickens with mud. Sunday speedboats buzz unseen below the bend where the brown water, slowly hovering, turns out of sight."

And of that oddly named country called Egypt (its original settlers were "reminded" of the ancient country) Bellow writes: "Between the Ohio and the Mississippi, Egypt lies low and hollow. Its streams are sluggish, old, swampy, and varicose. Spring floods bring fresh topsoil to many areas and the corn is thick. Toward Cairo the farmers make good cotton crops. We are here farther to the south than Richmond, Virginia. To a Northern nose, the air is slightly malarial. People's faces and their postures are Southern, and you begin to see things for which no preparation is possible."

Not even the briefest visit to the "Land of Lincoln"—as the state's automobile plates advertise Illinois—can end without bowing into its capital, Springfield, on the Sangamon River: the town Lincoln made his home; the place to which the President's remains were brought by train from Washington and where they were reverently enshrined. Around Springfield, now a city with a bustling population of well over eighty thousand, is the land, the flat prairie land, the circuit that Lincoln rode on horseback (sometimes by buggy) when he was practicing law; built up now, but not essentially beyond recognition.

Some fifty miles north is industrial and busy Peoria, on the Illinois River; and twice as far again, northeast, is Lake Michigan, the southern tip of it, a shoreline not dominated by birds and bird watchers, but by the soaring castles of steel, stone, and glass that make up Chicago's great skyline.

Not even a dot on the map when Marquette and Jolliet reached it in 1673 and a pile of ashes after the great fire of 1871, Chicago is (and long has been) the nation's second largest city, offering most of the urban delights—and problems—that New York does. Some say more! It is a hectic, ethnic, roaring city, the capital of the Midwest, brassy and extroverted and two-fisted, handsomely appointed along the Lake Shore Drive, teeming in its interior, second to none in the boldness of its downtown architecture, culturally awake, and a far cry from Carl Sandburg's biting description of "hog butcher to the world."

One arm of Chicago reaches almost into the pocket of Indiana's Gary; the other links the city to the closely strung lake-town suburbs from Evanston (with its Northwestern University) and Winnetka on up to Waukegan, and above that to Winthrop Harbor right by Wisconsin's border.

Iowa

The heart of the heartland, in the opinion of Paul Engle, a passionate admirer of the state. "Its greatest single force is dirt—fat dirt; out of its soil each year more wealth is produced than in all the gold mines of the world. Gently the land rises and falls, not flat, not broken into steep hills, but always tilting its fertile face to the sun. . . . Look at the map of Iowa, the Missouri wavering down the west side and the Mississippi down the east. Jutting eastward is a fine round pot belly, the broad Mississippi bending around it like a belt. For this is an abundant land."

Iowa, even more than Indiana, is a land of corn and hogs. It is a land of overpowering summers and savage winters, of short glittering springs when even the air smells like food, and of autumns, the harvest times, when the land yields up its staggering treasure. It is also a state of little valleys, few lakes, tiny streams, wooded slopes darkened with willow, elm, maple, hickory, black walnut.

It is a land with lyrical hills in the northeast called Tête de Mort, reminiscent, as are other French names in this territory, of the early white pioneers. And it is a land strong in Indian history, acknowledged in the names of counties, rivers, and towns in Iowa's north and west regions: Cherokee, Pocahontas, Pottawattamie, Sioux—and Sioux City, which looks across the river into Nebraska, above the Winnebago Indian Reservation.

Iowa's cities—among them Cedar Rapids, Dubuque, Waterloo, Mason City, Council Bluffs—are clean and charged with vigor; and its people are splendidly industrious and fair-minded. The largest city, the state capital (no Iowan ever pronounced Des Moines the way the French did, and do) is at the junction of the Des Moines River and the Raccoon River, well named and well combed by the early fur traders. The highest point in Iowa is Ocheyedan Mound, rising 1675 feet in Osceola County near the Minnesota border.

Between the two great rivers (the Mississippi and Missouri) Iowa balances, plagued by a furious physical climate, blessed by an abundant fertility, the loamy and unbelievably rich agricultural heart of the American continent.

Michigan

The Upper Peninsula, the romantic country of Hiawatha, is considered by many to be one of America's last great wildernesses; a place of pines and blue water and golden sands; a land of space and silence, and places, according to Gene Caesar, "wild enough to tingle the spine" with forests of green shadows, rocks like rainbows.

Moose are still sighted, coming down from Ontario, from the freeway leading into the vastness of the north woods; and Canada geese, in the Seney National Wildlife Refuge; and deer, in the swampy game preserve; and bears, which scarcely bother anyone. Wolf padmarks are occasionally seen in the snow; Caesar says, "If, as poetic outdoor writers so often insist, the howl of the timber wolf is the essence of the true wilderness, then Michigan's Upper Peninsula and its neighboring Wisconsin and Minnesota forests happen to be the only true wilderness this country has left outside of Alaska." But wolves do not find human beings particularly tasty.

Color and contrast in the Upper Peninsula: The dark-green country of the Tahquamenon River, an hour's drive west of Sault Ste. Marie. Clean air, vividly blue skies, clouds an intense white. This is unspoiled country, with two giant waterfalls—the upper, second only in size to Niagara—as well as a one-hundred-and-forty-five-mile-square labyrinth of swampland and wooded rises that comprise the Seney National Wildlife Refuge. Beyond is Lake Superior, its high sandstone cliffs sculptured into weird shapes that sometimes suggest battlefields and cathedrals—the "Sculptured Rocks" against the chill, white-beached austerity of the lake. The jutting and primitive Huron Mountains are found in the central region, and this is also copper country and a place of ghost towns.

Gene Caesar has advice for the traveler: "Leave the Copper Country . . . out of Houghton, jog on to the west along U.S. 45 through Ontonagon and Silver City to the Porcupine Mountains State Park, then top out on the escarpment and see the view of the Lake of the Clouds. You will forgive those who overwork the phrase 'God's Country' in describing the spot. Drop back down to continue along Michigan 28, and the Upper Peninsula's westernmost corner lies just ahead, nowhere surpassed for wilderness or scenery, particularly its white-water streams stair-stepped with cascades. Farther on, U.S. 2 comes up at Wakefield to offer an alternate route back to Mackinac Bridge, a route that includes some of the best areas for hunters and wild-flower photographers alike. Manistique offers a raft ride across a gigantic evergreen-bordered spring so clear that a penny can be seen sinking forty feet down and spooking the trout near the bottom."

Bruce Catton, a Michigan man to his bones, puts the final poetic touch to this "pleasantly melancholy" wilderness: "It is a strange country; lonely enough, even in summer, and cold as the far side of the moon when winter comes, with the far-off hills rising pale blue from the frozen white landscape. It offers a chance to draw a deep breath, to turn around and look back at the traveled path, to stand on a high hill and be alone with the fresh air and the sunlight. It is wood and water, golden sand and blue skies, emptiness and memories and the sort of isolation which it is hard for a city man to come by, these days."

How different it is in the Lower Peninsula. Across the southern part of the state lies the industrial might of America; the great network comprises Flint, Pontiac, Jackson, Lansing, Grand Rapids, and above all Detroit, the kingpin of the automotive industry. Detroit is big and sprawling and grimy and bursting with life; it is America's power center, the place where the weighty decisions are made, the kingdom of General Motors and Ford, and of hard-working millionaires who live baronially in suburbs like Grosse Pointe.

As Detroit produces and sells, so stands the economic health of the nation, and this city of money and muscle, the end product of the Industrial Revolution, couldn't care less about the past—which it preserves, nostalgically, in the immeasurably quaint Greenfield Village in Dearborn, the gift of Henry Ford, who invented the twentieth century.

Wisconsin

The haunting flavor of Michigan's Upper Peninsula persists and envelops the North Woods of Wisconsin—the rose-and-blue northland of marvelous winter sunsets, a frozen time of white beauty that is bequeathed only to the toughest. But the Big Woods of Upper Wisconsin are for the active and hardy, spring, summer, and fall. At the forty-fifth parallel a "disorderly Stonehenge" called "Ymer's Eyebrow" by the old Norsemen swings across the land, a stony, hard-bitten land, above which lies the Wisconsin of lakes and woods that mesmerizes city dwellers. In autumn the foliage turns the forest into what appears, from the air, to be a mass of zinnia beds. Lakes appear thickly, like floating islands.

In Oneida County, fishermen reel in black bass, scrappy walleyed northern pike, bluegills, and perch. Here German fairy-tale woods abound, and a feisty kind of German hospitality. Farther west, in and around Chippewa and Sawyer counties, are miles and miles of forest and great canoeing country. In summer, the muskie, fiercest of fresh-water fish, malevolent and unyielding, challenges the skill of every sportsman. It is the country of the fish story.

And nine thousand lakes! Crystal Lake, in the northwest, deep and true blue with water-lily pads floating on the top, has a dreamy quality, almost Southern; but an icy-bright light, sighing conifers, and the smell of balsam in the air. Nicolet National Forest, in far northeast Wisconsin is deep wilderness: high timber, shoulder-high bracken, the trails broken only by the sound of bird cries and the rippling of the water. Bass and black bears inhabit Butternut Lake, deep in the Nicolet Woods. Cranberry bogs are here and rice paddies strangely reminiscent of Sumatra, with Indians, silent and sliding through in their canoes, harvesting the brown grains of the delicacy known as wild rice.

Indians take care of their own reservation of forests in Menominee County, and in Door County—the thumb of Wisconsin that sticks sixty miles up into Lake Michigan —a rocky coast, birch and hemlock forests make "The Peninsula" a coveted place to live and vacation.

The northernmost north of Wisconsin is a red-sandstone archipelago extending out into Lake Superior—the Apostle Islands. This is country of Prussian-blue waters, high burgundy cliffs, green conifers, white birch, yellow beaches; thick forests and deep solitude, eagles and circling gulls. To the far horizon looms the Mesabi Range. It is the upper limit, the place where the northern lights explode and the loon keens on his evening flights, where the nights are mist-silvered, and where, Herbert Kubly says, one must have the "blessed strength to endure loneliness."

The largest lake in Wisconsin is in the east, below Green Bay—Lake Winnebago, with Oshkosh on its western banks. From here on down toward the Illinois border is the thickly populated area—more lakes, studded with villages, towns, and cities. Milwaukee, the largest city—famed for its brewing, meat packing, and shipping, and for its *gemütlich* atmosphere (a real German-American city)—marks the confluence of the Milwaukee, Menominee, and Kinnickinnic rivers, which empty into Lake Michigan. Racine also shares Lake Michigan; Madison, the capital, is between lakes Monona and Mendota; and Dam, appropriately enough, is by Lake Beaver.

But Wisconsin—let no vacationer, conservationist, or photographer heading north to the wilds of the state forget—is the dairy center of the United States, where the green and lush summer pastures yield dividends in cheeses that help make Wisconsin rich.

Minnesota

It has everything, geographically, that Michigan and Wisconsin can boast of— simply *more* so. It is not Midwest, but the opening door to the Northwest—so its citizens firmly state—and it is a bit larger than New England plus Maryland and New Jersey.

46

Minnesota has the big cities of Duluth and the twins, Minneapolis (the larger) and St. Paul (the capital). It has Lake Superior, and the Mississippi. It doesn't have mountains, but it does have tall bluffs along the rivers and these give a pleasing sense of height. It has more than eleven thousand lakes, it is the watershed of three river systems, Hudson Bay, Great Lakes—St. Lawrence, as well as the Mississippi—Missouri; and it is filled with marshes, swamps, sloughs, fens, muskegs, and bogs.

This is a melodramatic state with blue, arctic winters, brief and boisterous springs, summers that sparkle but are punctuated with horrendous storms, and a matchless Indian summer of wild blue skies, and ozone-scented air. The chain of wilderness lakes and rivers, streams and portages along the Canadian border—such as at Ely and the Superior-Quetico canoe country—is heaven to sportsmen, nature lovers, and escapists.

Here is the country of the Scandinavian settler, the dedicated worker, the enduring hard-muscled prosperous American who revels in fields carpeted with grain and who looks up to big skies and breathes in pure air. The great valley of the Red River in the north was once the place of the tall wild grass and herds of buffalo.

"You must see the prairies where they are perfect," writes Grace Flandrau of her state, "or you will not see them at all. There must not be the tiniest rise or fall of the earth, or your new sense of dimension will be lost. It must also be away from the centers of activity—out where the great farms are, and where the occasional group of grain elevators, the straight march of the telegraph poles, the rare, thin lines of planted trees are merely perpendicular lines that accentuate the total flatness." It is the other side of Minnesota, a strange opposition to the northern part of the profuse blue lakes, the great state and national forests, the Indian reservations, the remote beauty of lonely farms and pine-ringed fields and still ponds, and the lakes . . . the lakes . . . the lakes.

The Mississippi is a soul shaker. "And this is the state in which the 'Ole Man River' rises," writes Eli Waldron. "The Chippewas feared it and heard its roaring, though it does not roar. Dazzled by its wild radiance, they called it the River of Light. In the South the Indians called it the Big Strong. It had had other names as well—the St. Louis River, Buade River, Conception River, Colbert River, and the Rio del Espiritu Santo. The Ojibways called it *Misisipi*, from *misi*, meaning great, and *sipi*, river. Translated by an enthusiastic Frenchman, this came out as 'Father of Waters.' Whatever its name, to Americans it is *the* river. Pare Lorentz' memorable documentary about it, filmed during the Depression, is naturally titled just that—*The River*. Together with the Nile and the Amazon, it stands among the three greatest rivers on this planet."

From Lake Itasca in northern Minnesota to the Gulf of Mexico the Mississippi stretches 2,350 miles, ranking fifteenth among the world's great waterways. (The Missouri is actually longer by one hundred and sixteen miles.) It drains an area of 1,250,000 square miles—two-fifths of the United States—and thirteen thousand square miles of Canada.

Its water web stretches from the Rockies to the Appalachians, with two hundred and twenty-five miles of the Atlantic on one side and five hundred miles of the Pacific on the other. As Mark Twain observed, this is an area as great as the combined areas of England, Wales, Scotland, Ireland, France, Spain, Portugal, Germany, Austria, Italy, and Turkey. In the course of a year the Mississippi pours seven hundred and twenty-four billion cubic yards of water into the Gulf of Mexico, depositing in the process half a billion tons of silt, clay, sand, and gravel along a delta the size of Maryland and Delaware combined. Parts of Louisiana, Mississippi, Arkansas, Tennessee, Kentucky, and Missouri and as far north as Cairo, Illinois, came into existence this way.

"While the Upper Mississippi is sweet and feminine," Waldron writes, "the Lower Mississippi is powerful and masculine." It does not widen as it flows along; instead, it grows narrower and deeper. Beyond Cairo, nine hundred and sixty-four miles from the mouth, it flows in an alluvial valley banked by levees that rise above the surrounding land; one actually looks *up* at the river. On the Upper Mississippi you can look *down* at it from rock bluffs six hundred feet above the water.

The Mississippi is also a remarkably crooked river. Waldron declares, "Seeking to find a straight course, it often makes sudden cross-country leaps which leave some river towns stranded far inland, cause others to disappear and move parts of states from one side of the river to the other. Kaskaskia, once the capital of Illinois, disappeared in this fashion, as did Prentiss, Bolivar County, Mississippi, and Napoleon, Arkansas. Greenville and part of Vicksburg, Mississippi, once on the river, are now some distance away; Delta, Louisiana, once three miles below Vicksburg on a voyage down the river, now stands two miles *above* that city, owing to a cutoff. This tendency of the river to straighten itself out by cutting across the necks of looping bends has left the flood plain strewn with oxbow lakes from Memphis to the Red River. Here thirty or more crescent-shaped bodies of water, each five to ten miles long, roughly parallel the river's course for 500 miles. Thus the river is constantly in process of shortening itself."

THE PATHWAY TO THE WEST

Between the Midwest and the West are five adjoining states totaling over 376,000 square miles of vast prairie and grasslands, farms, desert land, rivers, and hills—and huge, huge expanses of sky. North and South Dakota, Nebraska, Kansas, and Missouri: a traveler from the east, heading out from St. Louis—a well beaten pathway to the West—would encounter these states, in approximately the opposite order. So for the sake of argument, let's start with Missouri.

At St. Louis, Eero Saarinen's soaring, magnificent archway proclaims that here, **Missouri** on the west bank of the Mississippi River, the West opens. Hundreds of miles away —on the east bank of the Missouri, the Big Muddy—Kansas City proclaims that it symbolizes the beginning of the true West. Small matter. Missouri was always the jumping-off place, and a stopping place. The pioneers, facing the dusty plains and deserts that lay between them and the Pacific, became attracted to the rich earth, the web of streams, the thick woods along the rivers, a fresh and new and hospitable land. Missouri is thus the oldest state west of the Mississippi.

It is a big state, larger than all New England, counterweighted by its two fine cities, with a lush northern prairie, good farmland (corn, soybeans, and wheat) and a booming vacation area in the Ozarks. It has a Southern mellowness in the region known as "Little Dixie," whose heart is Columbia and Boone County. German towns such as Hermann on the Missouri and southernish Louisiana on the Mississippi, hundreds of miles away, echo the days of gracious water traffic on both rivers. On El Camino Real, leading to St. Louis, the beautiful eighteenth-century town of Ste. Genevieve still seems to live through the Angelus rung out from the parish church.

St. Louis still has much of its Mississippi River flavor of the past, a city with Southern manners and Eastern hustle, with a lively journalistic tradition and well-kept homes, and with a passionate interest in jazz, baseball, and beer. Kansas City, on its bluffs above the Missouri River, is the quintessentially American city, clean, dynamic, cheerful—and busy, busy.

Florida and Hannibal have become touristy centers for the Mark Twain trade, and in northwest Missouri the natives have made a lucrative thing out of Jesse James. In Independence, Harry Truman's town, a surprising Victorian aura prevails.

But it is the Ozarks that beckon travelers to Missouri, fifty thousand square miles of mountains—America's oldest range—which spread beyond the state into Arkansas, Oklahoma, and Kansas. It is a land of lakes and hills, of rugged and gentle scenery, of quiet glens and roaring motorboat traffic. Once it was exclusively the domain of the hound dog, the fiddler playing at moonrise, of hillbillies and square dancing, of the Elizabethan ballad, a primitive survival of young America, Anglo-Saxon pure. Time, artificially created lakes, the influx of affluent sportsmen, and the building of many luxury accommodations have changed the rustic simplicity of the Ozarks. But it is still possible to find oases of the old unspoiled calm in the Taneycomo country and around Protem.

Of Kansas—"bloody" Kansas, which seemed to revive its accursed name after **Kansas** publication of Truman Capote's *In Cold Blood*—Debs Myers writes:
"The landscape is varied and so are the people. Far from being a flat and monot-

onous plain, Kansas rises nearly 3000 feet from east to west. The eastern part of the state is rich in hills, trees and water; the ground is lush and rolling. It is an area of small towns, farms, orchards and valleys. The western section of the state (closer to the public conception) is a vast, almost treeless land. The farms are large, and the population is spread thinly over prairies which stretch as far as a man can see. Yet to the people who live in western Kansas the land is good; the brooding immensity of the plains offers expansion and opportunity."

Hot summer winds, frigid winter blasts, terrible droughts, hungry grasshoppers —weather is the king that rules this part of the world:

"In Kansas, every man is his own weather prophet and the moods of the people are governed by the turning seasons. In the summer, when Kansas has the appearance of a grandmother's quilt patched with gold and green, there is an urgency about men and women as they watch the sky; for the harvest and their hopes are hitched to the wind, the sun and the rain. In autumn, if the harvest has been good, a festive confident feeling is apparent in the people; they seem to reflect the strength that has come from the bone marrow of the land. This quiet rejoicing finds an outlet in the dozens of farm expositions held across the state."

Nebraska

"Now, with Nebraska, where the Spanish explorer Coronado searched for gold in the land he called Quivira, the first glimmers of the sought-after West begin to appear. Nebraska is not only the prairie, cornbelt and wheatland state depicted in the popular mind; it's actually a tilted state, rising from 800 feet above sea level in the southeast corner of the state to Pine Ridge and the Wild Cat Range of the western border, a climb to 5400 feet in around 450 miles. It was this gradual climb toward the Continental Divide, with water and grass all the way westward—the direction the white man seems to move over the globe—that made the state the world's great path of empire."

The "path of empire." This startling image emerges from the pen of the late Mari Sandoz, a Nebraskan and descendant of the Sioux. In the miles of emptiness in the lush, rolling grasslands called the Sandhills, buffalo once grazed in teeming herds. To drive through this egg-shaped region is to see what Mari Sandoz called "the finest natural reservoir in the world—a great greenish-dun sponge that soaks up every drop of moisture from rain or snow and holds it in water tables and in the two thousand lakes." Here is a region of long, blue-hazed ridges, long valleys (one two hundred miles long), with fine stretches of meadow, long sweeps of yellow wild flowers, mats of bull-tongue cactus, yucca bloom, white gilly-flowers, and nests of prairie roses as large as one's palm.

Again in the words of Mari Sandoz: "Our first white-man highway was the spreading Missouri, but the Platte, flowing the length of the state from west to east, became the real path of empire across our prairie. Its course was followed by the fur men, then by the various Overlanders seeking home and safety and gold; by the Pony Express for a few profitless months, and by the telegraph and the first transcontinental railroad, until the broad river valley lay worn and bald, bare, it seemed, of every living root."

The state of Wild Bill Hickok, Buffalo Bill Cody, and the search for gold (Nebraska has no gold mines but many stories of buried treasure), the state of early violence and murder. Omaha, the largest city in the state (Lincoln is its capital) was founded as recently as 1854 with the opening of the Nebraska territory, and it grew rapidly as a supply point for pioneers heading west.

Today, Nebraska has sanctuaries for migratory waterfowl, the oil-and-grain-rich Panhandle, and in the northwest the bluffs and buttes of the old Sioux and Cheyenne stamping grounds, in addition to the moody and golden Niobrara Valley. Painters have always been tempted by the "swift, subtle flow of blue hazes against the Nebraska hills, the yellow-greens, the tans, russets, and mauves of the rolling prairie, the patterns of the contoured fields, and the unsurpassed sunrises and sunsets over it all," as Mari Sandoz describes it.

Nebraska and the Dakotas were once the great grazing grounds of the buffalo, that ill-fated animal symbolic of both Western romance and white man's greed. Has any other animal ever been slaughtered with such careless and brutal lack of concern? In Africa, perhaps, big game have suffered a similar fate. Buffalo hunting and buffalo slaughter undoubtedly had their economic uses, but the wholesale killing of the animal still provides a bitter, gory footnote to the story of the opening of the West. The virility cult of the Westerner presumably played an active role, and one wonders if Buffalo Bill, said to have killed and skinned a dozen buffalo a day, was the hero that legend claims for him. Mari Sandoz presents an indelible impression of what the West was like when the buffalo were left free to roam:

"Nebraska was once the richest of buffalo ranges, with its excellent waterways, the thick seedy June grasses and the later bluestems that stood more than man-high and could always be tromped out of the deepest snow. The great herds moved like vast dark shadows over the prairie, deer bounding away at their approach, antelope fleeing in droves, while plovers, curlews, prairie chickens and the great black ravens rose everywhere before the thunder and shake of the earth as the buffalo neared. Wild turkeys kept out of their way and flew in heavy whirring clouds through the golden sun of evening to their roosting groves in the brakes that the heavy-shouldered buffalo liked to avoid. The elk and moose usually kept to broken timbered slopes too. The bighorn sheep was all through Pine Ridge and the Wildcat range of the Panhandle and eastward, his great head dark against the clouds as he looked over the swift waters of the Niobrara striking the rolling flank of the Missouri like an arrow from the west.

"No gun roared anywhere then, and no stink of powder offended the nose. True, wolves and sometimes mountain lions pulled down any straggling buffalo, and half naked brown men crept up on the herds, stampeding them over the sheer bluffs of the upper White River country and along the Niobrara. With the women and children to help, they drove the buffaloes into pits or into gully or canyon surrounds.

"The white man's lead and powder worked faster, and when the herds were only white bones on the prairie or piled in ricks like tardy snowdrifts along the railroad tracks, the longhorns came trailing out of Texas, climbing from one stream to another to the Union Pacific railhead."

Nebraska has the healthiest climate in the United States, according to research done by John Younger Dickinson. The healthiest place is a stretch of Nebraska prairie south of the Platte River (but nobody knows why), a place of tall, windswept grass, corn, and cattle. "It's super-healthy in the villages and towns which lie in the valleys of Nebraska's so-called Big Blue and Little Blue rivers. . . . Any place in the Great Plains area, from Minnesota to western Texas, a man has a good chance of being around for his golden wedding anniversary, but he stands a better chance of enjoying it in this stretch of Nebraska—no matter whether he's poor or rich."

North Dakota
South Dakota

Nebraska, in one sense, seems only a preamble to the Dakotas. A vast, sometimes frightening, incredibly beautiful land, perhaps the last of pioneer America, a region barren of everything but beauty—so it was recently described, and its admirers (hundreds of thousands, millions even) claim that nothing much has changed or ever will. The two states are lumped together because, as Jack Schaefer, the noted writer of *Shane*, pugnaciously says, "Dakota is one piece, one place, one area. The very name, common to both states, defies the split. 'Dakotah' is a Sioux word meaning 'united.'"

Jack Schaefer explored this region in depth some years ago, and nobody has probed it with more of a sense of its romantic yet hard-boiled reality. He characterizes Dakota as follows: "148,000-plus square miles of prairie and plain and Badlands and a shading of hills called mountains and a patch of mountains called hills; a huge chunk of territory averaging more than 350 miles in width and more than 400 miles in height on the map, bigger even than the great bull-shaped expanse of Montana, topped in extent only by Texas and California. By size, and more important, by topography, Dakota is the biggest batch of wide-open spaces in the United States. Only Texas could dispute that—and the wide-open spaces of Texas are of a different, less impressive caliber."

The burly Missouri halves this rectangular piece of real estate, and history always seems close at hand in this vastness; fur trade and river traffic, Indian wars and gold rushes, land booms and speculation fever, all seem like yesterday's news. From a lofty bluff high over the Missouri where it unites with the Grand—close by the obelisk memory to Sacajewa, the Indian woman guide to the Lewis and Clark expedition—is the grave of Sitting Bull, the last tragic warrior to fight uncompromisingly against the white man. Cowboys and Indians still whoop it up for the tourists at Deadwood, and at Mandan you are suddenly gripped by the realization that this is it, this is where the great western high plains begin. Down a bit, on the west bank of the Missouri, is where—bands playing and banners flying—General Custer set out from Fort Lincoln for that unforgetable rendezvous on the Little Big Horn in Montana.

The Red River Valley in the northeast, shared with Minnesota, is deluxe farm-land country, golden in harvest time. The great Dakota prairie, with its buffalo (in the Theodore Roosevelt National Memorial Park, North Dakota), spreads eastward over to the wide Missouri—"that great glacial drift, rolling, treeless sea of soil left in ages past by the recurrent sheets of ice that crept down out of the north and leveled off the high places and filled in the low, and melting in defeat along the edges, created the Missouri Trench for the modern river."

A pleasant break in the prairie country comes with the sight of lakes and ponds and stretches of marshland, in northeast South Dakota and on up into North Dakota. But back to the prairie, a "natural grassland . . . settled, tamed, plowed, broken to harness. . . . As you push out into this prairie along any of the main east-west routes that slice across it, a sense of the land creeps in and grows until it dominates all else. The few farm buildings merge into their surroundings, natural objects in a natural world, and there is only the land, apparently limitless, serene, indifferent, enduring the surface scratchings of man, under the great rounded bowl of the sky. . . . The day wanes and the sun drops to the horizon and an unbelievable glory of color claims the sky. The people of wooded or hilly or mountainous country do not know what sunsets are."

West of the Missouri, the Dakota plain—rolling country marked by twisted and lonely buttes. It is the country of the Badlands, straddling the two Dakotas. "They cannot be described," Jack Schaefer writes, taking a bold stab at description, "those freakish, unearthly jumbles of ridges and hummocks and sharp cliffs and buttes, of domes and pyramids and cones, a weirdly lovely shape out of an artist's nightmare, striped in the browns and reds and grays and yellows and black of the pressed sand and clay and lignite of which they are formed . . . colors shifting in shade and tint with the shifting light and the play of the shadows. They cannot be described. Many people have tried—and the words limp behind the reality. They cannot even truly be held in mind. No matter how often seen, there are areas that always strain belief, are more weird and wonderful than remembered. Hell with the fires burnt out, General Sully described them long ago. That—or a drunken surrealist's dream of paradise."

Lastly, there are the Black Hills. Not hills, but mountains, solid and honest mountains, with superb spruce and pine forests seen from the surrounding plain. Geologists say they are the world's oldest mountains; they are indisputably beautiful, and one of America's newest playgrounds. An encircling view can be had from either Harney or Terry peak.

To the far horizon the plain of the Dakotas stretches to the wide Missouri, beyond is the great prairie, and beyond that, for miles and miles, is the Red River Valley. In the Black Hills natural wonders are for the asking: Spearfish Canyon, a long stretch of winding, cliff-lined magnificence; Custer State Park, where buffalo and antelope are still at play; Sylvan Lake; Wind Cave National Park. And of course, there is Mount Rushmore, still unbelievable, still the colossal memorial of all the fifty states, where the granite faces of four great Presidents—Washington, Jefferson, Lincoln, and the first Roosevelt—gaze with symbolic vision over Dakota, the state where the land, not man, still predominates.

THE ROCKIES

Indisputably, the Rockies are the greatest region of natural beauty in America, an awesome panorama of magnificent parks and forests, natural wonders, primeval areas, wilderness, lordly mountains, rivers, wildlife, immense skies, blessed space. They express the American heritage, the citizen's trust; they stand as the symbol of the hungering spirit, of the total grandeur of the youthful continent.

A. B. Guthrie, Jr., a mountain man from Chouteau, Montana, and author of *The Big Sky*, wrote that the Rocky Mountains were "not always in the knowledge or even in the imaginations of the pale invaders of the continent, yet there they were—known to the Indians, unknown to the whites, who became aware of them finally but couldn't believe in the unbroken mountain wall as they pushed for a passage to the islands of spice."

Peak after peak pierces the high, thin air like sharks' teeth. Lakes flow undisturbed in mile-high, alpine settings. Figures in the wide and stretching landscape appear ridiculously puny. Cascades roar down from the mountains, wildlife such as elk and coyote manage their immemorial struggle for survival, ghost towns send romantic chills up the spine, Indians still play out their non-TV destiny, silence is a gift for the asking. Even the desert is part of the Rockies.

The mountain men, the explorers, the settlers, the adventurers—Kit Carson, Jim Bridger, Lewis and Clark—the trappers, the gold seekers, the cowboys and Indians are the very stuff of American literature. It is the country of heroes as well as stereotypes. "Every nation has a national myth," R. L. Duffus writes, "without which it would not be a nation, but a mob. The open spaces in America are the symbol of our myth"—and of our ineradicable sentimentality for what we choose to believe is the pure and unspoiled.

Clifton Fadiman, who once made a study of the literature of the region, summed up the spatial meaning of the Rockies in the following manner:

"As James Bryce pointed out in 1888, of all the American regions, the Rocky Mountain domain is the one that most resolutely refused to face Europe, a fact that gives it its decisive and fascinating character—for there are few feelings more interesting than a sense of alienation from our origins: it made the clipper ship assume in our minds the profile and rhythm of poetry. We feel also that, though the cowboy and the cattle rustler are waxworks, the peaks and gulches and canyons and deserts still harbor loners, hermits, free artists, eccentrics, rockhounds—not a large population, it may be, but magnetic in their negative stance toward our electronic century.

"The place is so big, after all, that it can still hold out the lure of the unknown. Legends of buried treasure abound in the Rockies. The Superstition Range in the Sonora Desert has never been completely explored. Not many of us, no matter how fast we turn ourselves into camera-carrying tourists, have seen the mysterious Medicine Wheel deep in Wyoming, which is said to be as impressive as Stonehenge. . . .

"The American imagination . . . continues to cry out, almost in pain, surely in longing, for something visible and tangible, yet vaster, more enduring, more awe-inspiring, in a sense, than a human being. . . . A petrified forest can still give us the eerie thrill, and so can the Grand Canyon, the Painted Desert, the impossible world of the cacti, the endless spectrum of sapphires, coral, lead, agate, jasper, garnet, opals, galena, amethysts; the sudden flowering, like a bomb, of the desert; the Carlsbad Caverns; Wyoming's Pacific of grass; peaks, canyons, gulches, mesas, glaciers, geysers. To Americans all this is more than scenery. If you want scenery, you can do better along the Rhine. But the Rhine is too touched with history, too littered with the detritus of mankind, to give us what the Rockies can still give us: an intimation of Space that has escaped Time."

The Rocky Mountain states are Arizona, Colorado, Idaho, Montana, Nevada, New Mexico, Utah, and Wyoming, almost one million square miles of territory, surely staggering enough to boggle the imagination of even a Rhinelander. A. B. Guthrie, Jr., is, like most Western writers, almost tongue-tied before the glory of the West:

"The mountain states are plains—high plains—and peaks and valleys and air such as no one breathed before. They are deserts where, to borrow another writer's words, sunset lingers like the sound of golden horns. They are grasslands and forests. They are wild gentian and bear grass and mountain asters and yucca and sagebrush and prickly poppies and tiger lilies and aspen and alder and mesquite. They are mountain lions and bears and bobcats and rabbits and kit foxes and horned toads and rattlesnakes. They are the flutter of grouse and quail and the wing whistle of wild ducks heard at night. They are wrens and road runners and great golden eagles. In spite of scattered towns, big and small, they are distance and space, and they work for peace of mind."

The Rockies are young and violent, exuberant, challenging; they climb erect and sheer. Cliffs, glaciers, and gorges impede the intrepid climber. Sometimes their streams turn into torrents The rest stops are called parks or holes, like Pierre's Hole and Jackson's and Brown's—"score of places, some little known, many untenanted, where a man, exhilarated by his venturing, catches his breath, and, gazing on wild majesty, can imagine his feet stand where no feet stood before," Guthrie writes

"High plains and mountains may diminish a man," he continues, "making him a mite against immensity, and that is good; or they may enlarge and liberate him, and that, too, is good. In either case he finds kinship to the universe, finds himself a part of mystery and matter, a sentient bit of the great, elusive sentience that most men believe in and forever seek."

Highlands and mountains, stars so bright that they appear like campfires in the sky, height and distance without true reckoning, the feeling of closeness to the eternal mystery, the Westerner himself on the very top of life. The Rockies, as Guthrie says, can only be a feeling.

Another synonym for the American West is, of course, the Continental Divide, the spine of the continent. It is a ragged line running from the Mexican border, below Silver City, New Mexico, all the way beyond Glacier National Park, Montana, into Canada. It winds along impossibly high ridges and peaks, through winter snow barrens where man has never set an imprint, where rivers begin, where people are so scarce as to be almost invisible, through fertile grain and livestock country, through stark terrain where nothing lives, along eroded and fissured landscape where ice and wind have produced fantastic carvings, through bald and forested mountains, high passes, valleys, hills, and always more peaks. Neil Morgan plots the route:

"It comes up out of the desert of the Mexican state of Chihuahua and the Sierra Madre, and it picks up the first upthrustings of the Rocky Mountains in southwest New Mexico. It plods along a desert waste east of Navajo country . . . then it sprints west of Santa Fe and Taos and soars into the San Juan mountains of Colorado. For more than 300 miles it moves northward along one mountain range and then another, sometimes almost three miles high. To the west, rain and melting snow run off to the Colorado River, which cuts across the Southwest desert on its way to the Gulf of California and out to the Pacific. To the east, the flow is to the Arkansas or the Platte, and on to the Mississippi and the Gulf of Mexico.

"Then the Divide, coasting down out of the Front Range of the Rockies into the Red Desert of Wyoming, seems to rest awhile. The Oregon Trail crossed the Divide at South Pass (meeting the Overland Trail), and the wagon ruts are still there between the stony buttes. From South Pass you see only the high prairie; sometimes a sheepherder's wagon or a pair of antelope. . . .

"Now the Divide rides the Wind River Mountains north past Jackson Hole into Yellowstone, winding through the geysers in a circle that befuddled the frontiersmen. . . . Beyond, it serves its only stint as a state border, between Idaho and Montana. Then it turns from the Bitterroot Range to embrace the Big Hole country of Montana. It straightens away through Butte, extending up the Lewis and Clark Range at the edge of the big-sky flatlands to Glacier Park and the Canadian Rockies. Here, finally, the waters of the Divide no longer belong alone to the Atlantic and Pacific; the Arctic Ocean joins the watershed of the Divide."

Colorado

Montana, Idaho, Wyoming, Colorado, Utah, Nevada—these, for our purposes, are the six states of the Western Tier. Begin with Colorado, the state with the lordly scenery, the state that many people feel is the ideal American state, end to end. Denver, the state capital, at the foot of the Front Range; Colorado Springs, at the foot of the Rampart Range; Pueblo and Canon City, near the Wet Mountains—all are starting points for the traveler heading west to see the Rockies, nature's dazzling scenic blowout.

Colorado boasts six hundred mountain peaks more than twelve thousand feet high, three hundred peaks more than thirteen thousand feet high, and fifty-two mountains that stretch above fourteen thousand feet. It is a state of two-fisted rivers, glacial canyons, lakes on the flat tops of mountains, tiny streams, even a desert created from the sands of a vanished inland sea. It is a state of the earned superlative, of emptied and romantic mining ghost towns, of beloved Pikes Peak (not the highest, even at 14,110 feet), and high culture at Aspen; of dutifully visited attractions such as the Garden of the Gods in Colorado Springs, the Royal Gorge of the Arkansas River, the primitive Indian dwellings in Mesa Verde National Park, the sheer walls of the Glenwood River rising one thousand feet above the boiling Colorado River, the raw, primitive scenery of the Red Mountains, saw-toothed masses of stone, and of the bony, sunset-struck peaks of the San Juan Range.

It is a big, lavish, even frightening state. It is rapturous country. Handsome, open skiing at Vail and Aspen typifies the exuberance of the true West, that deeply gratifying feeling that space is big, wide, never-ending, overgenerous, that man is free to ride with the wind, soar, open himself at last to *space*. Exuberance, open-handedness, expansive skies—Colorado is almost an introduction to the Western experience, the Western imagination, the Western casualness of life and living with nature in the grand and in the raw. "And men shall fashion glaciers into greenness/ And harvest April rivers in the autumn." So reads the inscription on the walls of the State House in Denver, a statement and a prophecy.

At the Mesa Verde National Park, in the corner of Colorado overlooking Arizona, New Mexico, and Utah, there is another message: Indian civilization is real and identifiable; from here moving westward an American must realize that the Indian has been a strong and palpable factor in the West. Indeed, he was so long before the West was

56

first seen by the white man. Mesa Verde is a green tableland—fifty thousand acres of canyons and mesa lands, excavated ruins and cliff dwellings of Indians who, along with their culture, vanished long ago. Debs Myers writes:

"Archeologists have pieced together a partial history of these people—who they were, where they came from, where they went. Yet much of it is still a mystery and probably will remain so. That, perhaps, is a basic reason why it exerts such a powerful attraction. . . . About 800 years ago, the cliff dwellers deserted their homes and vanished. There have been varied theories as to why this happened: plague, superstition, or a surprise attack that resulted in annihilation. The archeologists shake their heads to this; they attribute this mass exodus to a great drought which they believe afflicted the Southwest from 1276 to 1299; year after year the crops withered until the cliff dwellers lost heart and moved out of Mesa Verde.

"Before they left, probably heading deeper into the west, they built on the mesa top a curious walled structure known as the Sun Temple. The accepted theory is that this ancient temple, built around intricate passageways and kivas (underground ceremonial rooms), was intended to placate the Sun God and to bring a merciful end to the drought. The temple was never completed. Why? No one knows, of course; perhaps because the people lost faith in the promises of their medicine men.

"That is only one of the riddles. Where did the cliff dwellers find refuge when they made the long journey in search of water, what is the significance of the peculiar structure of the Sun Temple, what strange rituals took place in the underground ceremonial chambers? The answers—one guess is as good as another."

In Wyoming, as we shall soon see, there is another and perhaps even more thrilling Indian mystery. The West, even today, still abounds in them.

Wyoming

New: the state became part of the Union even later than Colorado, fourteen years later; in 1890. Old: the ageless hills and mountains, the cities, among them Cheyenne (Wyoming's capital), Casper, Laramie—names that create mind pictures of filmdom's West.

To the east of Colorado is the river of grass; to the north and west, the Tetons, Yellowstone, the Big Horn, and Wind River, scenery almost monotonously described as magnificent, breathtaking, awesome, fabulous. But grass is the central fact of Wyoming. First the buffalo followed the grass, then the Indians followed the buffalo; and the cattlemen followed the Indians. Literally, the state of Wyoming has sprung, although the term may be hackneyed, from "grass roots." Blue grasses, wheat grasses, fescues, redtops—there are more than one hundred and fifty varieties to be found.

Blissfully underpopulated, the mountainous source of three great river systems—the Columbia, the Colorado, and the Missouri—this state is marked by vastness and solitude. "Nearly everything else," Bernard De Voto once said, "is scenery, emptiness, and the ever-enduring grass. The characters in the cavalcade of Wyoming—the Indians, the trappers, the miners, the scouts, the bullwackers, the mule skinners, and the cowboys—left hardly a trace in their passing. They came, they did, and they went." Wyoming, despite the summer influx of hordes of tourists, remains what it has always been: a grazing state.

Wyoming occupies so much room—it is seventy-eight times the size of Rhode Island—that even the scenery is sometimes hard to find. The state is, geologically, a big, high mesa; the average altitude is six thousand feet. The great mountain ranges—the Big Horns, the Tetons, the Wind Rivers, and the Absarokas—are actually outthrusting peaks of the mesa. They can be found in the north and west; Struthers Burt, who wrote about Wyoming in *Powder River*, said that "they go and hide themselves." And De Voto has quoted a pithy native: "They ain't hankering after company." But through Wyoming is threaded the path of American history.

Consider the Medicine Wheel, found in the northern tip of the Big Horn Mountains; the Big Horns are in the north-central part of the state. It is one of the oldest works of man—comparable to the great slabs of Stonehenge, the giant statues on Easter Island, the terraced pyramids discovered in certain South Sea islands—and it may be that it is the very oldest man-made artifact on the North American continent. It is a hair-raising experience to get to it: out of Sheridan, ascending the Big Horns by means of switchbacks and hairpin curves (on a clear day, thirty miles from Sheridan, you can see the Black Hills, two hundred miles away) that climb to the glacial rubble known as "The Fallen City," past the tremendous outcropping of rock, the V-shaped "Steamboat Rock" (more like the Winged Victory in its soaring, airy lightness and sense of arrested flight), over a saddle of the Big Horn range (eight thousand feet high, now), passing through stands of pine and Engelmann spruce and Douglas firs, mountain meadows blooming with Indian paintbrush, harebells, gentians, lupine, touch-me-nots. The climb to the summit of the Big Horn (ten thousand and thirty feet), near the rock-domed Bald Mountain, and beyond—let Bernard De Voto pick up the narrative from here:

"When at last you gain the summit of the mountain on which the Medicine Wheel lies, nearly 10,000 feet high, you have the feeling, in those pure, clean reaches of the upper air, that you have made your way to the moral top of the world. You understand why the Indians held this place in reverence as Big Medicine; some atavistic stirring tells you that it is Big Medicine still.

"On top of the mountain, which levels off into a kind of small plateau and from which you can see for miles, there is an almost perfect circle made of rough, unhewed stones laid side by side. None of the stones is particularly large and no effort was made to fit them together. They were just laid there, one after the other, apparently as they came to hand. The circle, or wheel, is seventy feet in diameter and 245 feet in circumference. In its center is a mound of stones like a hub, three feet high, and twelve feet around, from which twenty-eight spokes radiate to the rim of the wheel. These spokes are also made of stones of varying shapes and sizes. Around the rim of the wheel, at irregular distances, are six stone mounds that are somewhat smaller than the one in the center. These now look like piles of rock that children at play might have heaped up, but when first discovered by the white man they were built up on three sides with the fourth side left open, after the fashion of an armchair. Five of the stone mounds had the open side facing inward toward the center of the wheel, and the sixth, which is on the east point of the compass, faced outward toward the rising sun. The mound in the center for many years supported a bleached buffalo skull, the eye sockets of which also looked to the east, but it disappeared some years ago.

"All that is known for certain about the Medicine Wheel is that it is ages old—so old that even the Indians have no legends about it. The Crows say that the wheel was there when their people first came to the Big Horns. The old men of the tribe say they do not know who built it; they say that the wheel was there 'before the light came' or 'before the people had iron.'"

The rest is scenery. Yellowstone, Jackson Hole, the Tetons, Shoshone National Forest, the Wind River Range, South Pass, Snow King Mountain—western Wyoming is the land of the giant picture postcard, views and panoramas, the spectacular sights. Can anything fresh be said about Yellowstone, except that its waterfalls are indeed mind blowing, its gorges impressive, its geysers faithful to their appointed eruption time, its volcanic craters suitably scary? Or about the Tetons, incontestably Wyoming's loveliest drawing card, with four hundred miles of the green, fertile valley of Jackson

Hole bounded by mountains on all sides, and its two lakes, Jackson and Jenny, indescribably beautiful. De Voto resumes:

"The name, 'The Tetons,' bestowed by French trappers who penetrated the area in the early 1800s, was originally attached to but three mountains—Grand, Middle, and South Teton. The Frenchman knew them as *Les Trois Tétons*; the blunt, forthright translation is 'the three teats.' An even earlier explorer, Wilson Price Hunt, called them the Pilot Knobs. An intrepid man, Hunt, but in this instance at least, a little too genteel. *Les Trois Tétons* won out over the Pilot Knobs. . . . They were first seen, however, by a fellow who didn't bother to do much christening, John Colter, the first white American to set foot in Wyoming. He got there in 1806."

Who was Colter—the forgotten man of Wyoming's, indeed the West's, history? De Voto explains: "An enlisted man under Lewis and Clark, he made his way with the expedition to the Pacific Coast, followed it back on the return journey to St. Louis as far as the mouth of the Yellowstone River, and then, meeting up with two trappers, he asked for and received his discharge. That was in August, 1806. Within a year, having tired of his partnership with the two other trappers and going it alone, he had rung up a long list of 'firsts'—first explorer of the Big Horn River and the country of the Big Horns; the first white man to cross Union and Teton passes; the first white man to see the headwaters of the Wind, the Snake, and the Green rivers; the first white man to pass through what is now Yellowstone Park; and the first white American to see the Teton Mountains, the Teton Basin, and Jackson Hole.

"Where Colter led, others followed, Jackson Hole, now a national monument, became a favorite rendezvous for the mountain men—it is named, incidentally, after one of them. So far as Colter's memory is concerned, there isn't a place in Wyoming that bears his name. And all he did was to discover it practically singlehanded.

"The mind-heart echoes of old trappers on the beavered stream. The grind of prairie schooners. A buffalo skull in a wallow. The time-gentled melancholy of the first homesteaders, forced to leave the sunsets. An arrowhead shining in the gravel after rain. Mountain water over shining rock. Stars like bonfires. Clouds swelling in the bellies of the peaks in Glacier Park. A cottontail at the edge of a thicket. A horseman and a bronc. Old Chief Big Lake's grave on a benchland facing westward over the valley of the Teton. Fishing streams and one trout rising to my Royal Coachman, and my not caring much if it should get away. A bar of song remembered from some country-schoolhouse dance. The wild geese V-ing, shouting their adventure. A buck's antlers through the quaking aspen. The first men here and the things they saw that I see now. The coyotes calling."

Montana

Ruminating in a cabin at Twin Lakes, "a pocket in the great eastern apron of the Rockies," A. B. Guthrie, Jr., a native, evoked the symbols of Montana, which strike a profound personal chord. It is a state that somehow gets deep to a writer; even John Steinbeck found it to his enormous liking:

"I am in love with Montana. For other states I have admiration, respect, recognition, even some affection, but with Montana it is love and it's difficult to analyze love when you're in it. . . . It seems to me that Montana is a great splash of grandeur. The scale is huge but not overpowering. The land is rich with grass and color, and the mountains are the kind I would create if mountains were ever put on my agenda. Montana seems to me to be what a small boy would think Texas is like from hearing Texans. . . . It seemed to me that the frantic bustle of America was not in Montana. . . . The calm of the mountains and the rolling grasslands had got into the inhabitants. It was hunting season when I drove through the state. The men I talked to seemed to me not moved to a riot of seasonal slaughter but simply to be going out to kill edible meat. . . . Love is inarticulate. Montana has a spell on me. It is grandeur and warmth. If Montana had a seacoast, or if I could live away from the sea, I would instantly move there and petition for admission. Of all the states, it is my favorite and my love."

Montana is big, big—nearly three times the size of the state of New York; rolling prairie in the east, sheep and cattle country, the Great Plains, where the climate can be hellish and the wind can set the teeth on edge. The vast wheat fields lie plowed and planted in the dry-farming pattern of green-and-black stripes, a wallpaper pattern. In the west are the mountains, the Rockies, and the larger cities; Great Falls, Helena (the capital), and Butte, near which is Anaconda with its copper mines.

This is a state of mines—zinc, coal, sapphires, silver, and gold, as well as copper— of ghost towns and the oddball gold prospector, still seeking a strike; a state for fishing and hunting, camping, dude ranches, skiing (Big Mountain is but one of many good runs); a state of wilderness area (the Bob Marshall) penetrable only on foot or horse; of the National Bison Range, the Lewis and Clark Cavern, and the broad and sturdy Missouri River.

Historically, Montana is "The Treasure State," as John D. Weaver observes: "It has been a rich, remote wilderness to loot and leave. The fur traders came for beaver, the prospectors for gold, the buffalo hunters for hides, the copper kings for plunder, the cowmen for the open range, the homesteaders for free government land. It was the custom to make a bundle in Montana, then move to Boston, New York, or Los Angeles and endow symphony orchestras, museums, and libraries."

And, of course, Montana has the magnificent Glacier National Park, the favorite of calendars and beer advertisements, the ultimate, perhaps, in the West's scenic amplitude of glaciers, boulders, Douglas fir and quaking aspen, roaring waterfalls, sprays of mist, rock-bordered lakes, Rocky Mountain goats, gorgeous wild flowers, deceptively friendly bears. "Give a month at least to this precious preserve," the naturalist John Muir wrote of the park. "The time will not be taken from the sum of your life. Instead of shortening it, it will indefinitely lengthen it." Clean and clear, the big sky of Montana watches over a seemingly boundless area that has haunted every American writer from Muir to Steinbeck.

Idaho

In the words of A. B. Guthrie, Jr.: "Idaho, they will tell you, means sunrise; and the sun, they will agree, must be astonished each time he lifts his bright face on the place. . . . Here is a land wrought by fire and ice, by the slow force of glacier and the eruptive energy of volcano, a land of rivers and deserts, of forests and of barrens, of mountains and flats, of sterility and fruitfulness, of cold zone and temperate, of growing settlement and eternal wilderness."

Idaho, which is just the width of Oregon (or of Washington, in its northern boundaries) from the Pacific Ocean, is a land of contrasts. In the north, for example, are mirrorlike Pend Oreille, a lovely trout-stocked lake, and the subalpine Coeur d'Alene and Priest; and southward, the "reaches of stone and dust that frazzled the fiber of man and beast in the days when men strained overland to Oregon," as Guthrie describes it. There are the potato fields (only Maine potatoes rival Idaho's), the wheat-farm district around Palouse and Potlatch—good to the last inch of soil—and the unyielding, rocky, lunar landscape of the Craters of the Moon near Arco. There is Boise, the state's capital and largest city, at the foothills of the Salmon River Mountains, and the Boise Valley, a fat and peaceful contrast to the torn waste of Owyhee County, a range land for antelope and wild horses. And there is the Snake, the Mad River of the French, aided by its little sister, the Salmon—"The River of No Return." Guthrie writes:

"Once the outlet for prehistoric Lake Bonneville—shrunk now to the comparative puddle of Great Salt Lake—the Snake goes its prehistoric, uncivilized way, now complacent, now raging, now gentle with its shores, now scouring deeper the chasms scoured long, long ago. Hell's Canyon, upriver from Lewiston, is the deepest gorge on the North American continent. Here, between walls of basalt, greenstone, rhyolite, and andesite, the Snake digs at a bed more than a mile below its rims." This is still the most thrilling ride on a small craft that it is possible to enjoy (with a large dose of sheer terror) on the continent.

Idaho was the state beloved by Ernest Hemingway, who now lies in his grave near Ketchum, in the Sun Valley area beneath the Sawtooth Mountains. Hemingway wrote fondly and well of his adopted state.

The Sawtooth Mountains bite into the skyline of south-central Idaho, with ten-thousand-foot peaks pricking the thin air like sharpened teeth. Glacial lakes endure in mountain hollows. Unfished streams flow without hindrance, no woodsman's ax cuts into the timber. North of Ketchum the upland valleys are reminiscent of the Pyrenees, the province of those faithful sheepherders, the Basques.

Idaho is full of gold camps and their buried tales and dreams. "Gold was a symbol," Guthrie says, "it was the wildwood hope, the ultimate ecstasy, the sum of dreams. Find it, and it is no more than greasy metal, and far off lies the strike that answers all, over the next mountain, in the next valley, on the shore of some secret stream."

The north of Idaho foreshadows the territory beyond in the Northwest: "What you notice first in northern Idaho," Guthrie observes, "are the noble stands of timber, of white and yellow pine, of larch and fir, of cedar and hemlock and spruce. They rise majestically, even awesomely, and you find yourself speaking quietly in the felt presence of the forest gods. Here and there are mills, and now and again big trucks come rolling by, laden high with fine, clean logs, and the air tastes of pitch and needle and sawn wood, and you feel humble and exhilarated and altogether good."

The nostalgia the American West nurtures comes from such names as Lochsa, Selway and Clearwater, Lemhi and Lost—"Names cradled by mountains, flanked by long plains. Names echoing yet the first wonder of men at the wonder of regions still wonderful. Lonely names, some of them, for places of good loneliness."

Utah

It might be said that Utah is the fantasy state of the Union, a gigantic stage set, a Panavision dream sequence out of a Walt Disney movie. It is the land of the Mormons —thrifty, shrewd, clean-living, and hard-bargaining—and it is one of the richest of all American states in natural wonders.

Utah is understandably proud of its breathtaking plains (at Promontory, for instance) and canyons, eroded shapes (as in the Goblin Valley), chasms and stone monuments, natural arches and tiers of painted cliffs, sandstone gorges, and wild tangle of plateaus and mesas. Utah is at least ninety per cent scenery and most of it is indeed staggering and moving. The state is also, if one is not a Mormon, a strange place of isolation. "This is a mountain island," writes native son Samuel W. Taylor, "and within its mental wall all is officially well."

Its natural wonders form a catalogue of some of America's most startling sights: Bryce Canyon, with its pink-limestone spires, domes, and arches, rising from the huge amphitheater's one-hundred-foot depth, the creations of millennia of wind and weather. The vista of the Colorado gorge at Dead Horse Point, "tier upon tier of rainbow cliffs to the end of vision," the living color of the stone blooming and fading and changing with the time of day. Arches National Monument, the great convulsions of the San Juan called the Goosenecks; the unbelievable Zion National Park; Canyonlands; Wayne

Wonderland; Natural Bridge; Monument Valley. The world-famous Bonneville salt flats and also, of course, the Great Salt Lake with Salt Lake City, Utah's capital (founded by the Mormons in 1847) at its southeast tip.

The scenic wonders of Utah have been monotonously described, raptured over, and photographed, but very little quality has emerged in the mechanical descriptions of these natural formations. The reason for this may be, as Taylor suggests, that Utah "is an island fairyland of enormous beauty, peopled by a unique brand of tightly knit Puritans." Perhaps the mind, stunned by these weird and psychedelic formations, loses the capacity to say anything fresh and meaningful about them. They are there; they should be seen; they have the effect of marvels and miracles. On the other hand, the Great Salt Lake, perhaps because of its very bizarreness, can prod a gifted writer like Wallace Stegner into a flight of almost poetic prose: "The world's strangest sea" is all that is left of what was once Lake Bonneville, a freshwater sea as big as Lake Michigan.

"On the face of the Wasatch Mountains, and on the faces of the tormented desert ranges westward," Stegner writes, "there are lines of terraces like the grades of abandoned roads. The highest is a thousand feet above the floor of the valley. Up there the soil is underlaid with flattened, polished stones: the beach of a great lake that in glacial times pushed against this eastern wall of the Great Basin. It made fiords of the Wasatch canyons and a great bay of the Cache Valley. Westward it spread more than a hundred miles, submerging low mountains and making islands of high ones. Northward it reached four arms into what is now Idaho; southward, a long bay almost touched present Arizona. This was Lake Bonneville. . . .

"Stand on its highest terrace and count the ledges, in places only a few, in places several dozen, that the receding waters cut in the mountainous shore. Some are so faint that a heavy growth of grass obscures them; some so broad and deep they indicate a stable level over thousands of years. And away westward twenty-five miles or more, against the foot of brown mountains and island, you can see what is left of that inland sea—a thin line of quicksilver, of lead, of improbable turquoise, of deep-sea cobalt, or of molten metal, depending on the condition of the sky: Great Salt Lake."

It is the biggest lake west of the Mississippi, a bizarre and contradictory phenomenon; not a single oasis stands in this area of water seventy-miles long and fifty wide, and its nonsink swimming is highly overrated. Stegner ponders:

"It is a desert of water in a desert of salt and mud and rock, one of the most desolate, and desolately beautiful, of regions. Its sunsets, seen across water that reflects like polished metal, are absolutely unrivaled. Its colors are of a staring, chemical purity. The senses are rubbed raw by its moonlike horizons, its mirages, its parching air, its moody and changeful face."

And in Bear River Bay, at the north end of the Great Salt Lake, at the mouth of the lake's principal tributary, is such a concentration of wildfowl as to make even more forbidding the desolation out beyond; a place to set the devoted bird watcher gaga.

Nevada

Very West, and vast in its Westness, Nevada is a place of gloomy mountain ranges and desolations of desert, of crumbling and deserted towns. It is also the setting of Las Vegas and Reno. But the state is also heir to the great traditions of the West—mining, ranching, farming, hunting, fishing. Space, in illimitable abundance, forms the background for individualism, gambling fever—and emptiness.

Lucius Beebe, who adopted Nevada as his home state and reactivated Mark Twain's famed *Territorial Enterprise* in that sweetest of all Nevada towns, Virginia City, once wrote: "The scenery of Nevada and its at times plutonian landscape—rivers that run to no sea, endless sage, geologic formations that would have interested Dante—are a far cry from the pretty pastorals of New England, the garden vistas of the Deep South or the conventional snowcapped peaks of the mountain states. To the first settlers who forged their way westward over unchartered trails to California, the Golden, Nevada was all a part of the 'Great American Desert,' implacably grim, hostile, a land of death and of legends of death."

Yet of that great space: "Claustrophobia is an ailment unknown in the Nevada lexicon. There is space to swing a cat, to fall down in if one wishes. The native Nevadan will tell you that the moon rises in more incredible fullness over the Great Salt Lake Desert or Toiyable National Forest or the Washoe Hills, as the case may be, than anywhere else on earth. The sunset shadows creeping across the chocolate ice-cream hills form shapes of history instantly discernible to the perceptive eye. The past is very close indeed in Nevada, and to the ear attuned to the vibrations of the Western continent the sound of stagecoaches on the night wind and the rattle of gunfire are reality and not illusion."

Here is romance tinged with a hard-headed sense of the truth, and in the desert-and-mountain-surrounded towns of Virginia City, Elko, Carson City (the state capital), Mindon, and Austin, the gamblers generously allow Nevadans to enjoy an uncommonly spacious and uninhibited way of life.

The desert and desert life of the West attract gritty loners, mad prospectors, and poets, such as Walter Van Tilburg Clark. The Spanish padres and the conquistadors were afraid of the Nevada desert, the wasteland with its wide, flat stretches of barrens that lead the eye toward all but lifeless mountains in the distance, and where even the Joshua tree seems to lift its branches in supplication! Two images come to mind: the terrible, punishing pain inflicted on the pioneers and the weeks it took them to cross the desert; the joke-in-truth of the grizzled prospector standing beside his dead burro and eyeing a post that announces a hundred miles to water, fifty miles to wood, a million miles to God, three feet to hell. Yet, writing of this "colorless monotony, the interminable gray brush, the white, blinding stretches of the sinks and the dry lakes," Walter Van Tilburg Clark seeks to penetrate the mystery of this grim landscape:

"No desert makes many quick converts, and the Nevada desert has less about it that is picturesque and various, in a conspicuous way, than most. It is like ocean in its effect upon mind and spirit, and not only by its great, stony waves of mountains and troughs of empty valleys. The power of its extent and its monotony to remind a man of his own significance and brevity is like that of the ocean. As with ocean, only changes of light and weather can make any considerable difference in it, and even these differences do not change the dominant suggestion of the eternally unconcerned. . . . While crossing Nevada, there is some fear, some apprehension of loss of self, which is like the fear, the diminishment, many feel when they look at the sea. And desert does not have the attraction of source, the power to draw one back to itself, that is in the ocean. There is none of that sense of returning to one's home place, that stirring of long, melancholy but entrancing sensations of having been there and not quite altogether forgotten the experience. The desert does not move either. It does not stir or make a sound. It has no rhythm but the visible, static rhythm of its shapes. So, altogether, it is more complete, more remote, more appallingly indifferent than ocean is to the nagging, necessary little human sense of self-importance."

The fear and attraction of the desert—like any other human mystery, only those who live with it can understand it. In Nevada, Clark says, no town is big enough to shut out the knowledge of the desert and the kind of special history the desert begets, and Nevadans, the desert dwellers, can communicate only to their own kind their personal love for it.

(*Text continued on page 162*)

1. Summer along the coast of Maine. ►

2. Seals and gulls near Pemaquid Point, Maine. ► ►

4. Dunes at Wellfleet, Cape Cod, Massachusetts.

3. Gay Head, Martha's Vineyard, Massachusetts.

5. Menemsha Harbor, Martha's Vineyard, Massachusetts.

7. Manchester, Vermont.

6. Inland Massachusetts; the glory of a New England autumn.

8. Winter in New England: Dixville Notch, New Hampshire.   9. Christmas time at Lyndon, Vermont.

10. In the Green Mountains, near St. Albans, Vermont.

11. Church at Manheim, in the foot-hills of New York's Adirondacks.

12. Niagara Falls. ►

13. Wickford, on Narragansett Bay, Rhode Island.

14. Seaport at Mystic, Connecticut

15. Midtown reflections, New York City. ▶

16. The Tempe Wick House, Morristown, New Jersey.

17. Pond at Birchrunville, Pennsylvania.

18-20. Pennsylvania Dutch farm at Intercourse.

22. Fountain at the Philadelphia Museum of Art.

◄ 21. Independence Hall (and Independence
Square), Philadelphia, Pennsylvania.

23. Farm near Millersburg, Ohio.

24. Autumn at Chillicothe, Ohio.

25. Canadian geese check in at Oxford, Maryland.

26. The Washington Monument, Washington, D.C.

27. The Lincoln Memorial, Washington, D.C. ►

29. Springtime near Charlottesville, Virginia.

28. Westover, in Virginia's James River country.

30. Bluegrass country: "Calumet Farm," near Lexington, Kentucky. ▶

◄ 31. Along the Blue Ridge Mountains — in North Carolina.

32. Key Deer, Weeki-Wachee Forest, near St. Petersburg, Florida.

33. Beach scene at Pensacola, Florida. ►

34. "The Shadows," plantation at New Iberia in Louisiana.

35. On the Ohio River; heading northeast from the Mississippi toward Louisville, Kentucky.

36. Farmland in Oklahoma's Comanche County.
In the distance are the Wichita Mountains.

37. Winter landscape in Kansas. ►

38. Prairie, near Chenoa, Illinois. ► ►

40. Lake Michigan, near Heron Bay.

39. Chicago, Illinois. Looking down Wacker Drive.

42. Farm near Coon Valley in Vernon County, Wisconsin.

41. Cove on Lake Superior,
near Marquette, Michigan.

43. Burntside Lake, near Ely, Minnesota.

44. Superior-Quetico canoe country in Minnesota.

◀ 45-46. Buffalo on the Great Plains. And a plowed field near Winner, South Dakota.

47. Pack trip, along the Gros Ventre Mountain Range, Wyoming. ▶

49. Gulls over Utah's Great Salt Lake.

48. Old Faithful, Yellowstone Park, Wyoming.

50. Rainbow over Promontory, Utah. ►

51. Goblin Valley, near Hanksville, Utah. ► ►

52. San Juan Mountains, near Durango, Colorado.

53. Bell Mountain, near Aspen, Colorado.

54. The Rio Grande River. Borderline between
Texas and Mexico, near El Paso and Juárez. ▶

55. Cowboy in the sand hills near
Monahans, east of the Pecos, Texas.

56. White Sands National Monument, near Alamogordo, New Mexico. ▶

57. Looking toward the San Andres Mountains, New Mexico.   58. San Miguel Mission, Santa Fe, New Mexico. ►

59. Canyon de Chelly National Monument, Arizona. ► ►

60. Sheepherders in Monument Valley, Arizona.

61. Navajos in Monument Valley. ▶

62. San Xavier Mission, near Tucson, Arizona. ▶ ▶

64. Joshua Tree National Monument, near Indio, California.   65. Yosemite National Park, California.

66. Point Lobos, south of Carmel, California. ►

67. San Francisco, viewed through the Golden Gate Bridge.

68. Cliffs near Nesika Beach, Curry County, Oregon. ▶

◄ 69. Farm near Potlatch, Idaho.

70. Black-tailed deer, near
Mt. Rainier in Washington.

71. Glacier National Park, Montana. ►

72. Big Mountain, near Whitefish, Montana.

73. Wildflowers in Washington's Olympic National Park.

74. Surfing in Waimea Bay, Oahu, Hawaii. ▶

◄ 75. Lynn Canal, between Haines and Skagway, Alaska.

THE SUPERSTATE

Texas

Most Americans, including even the most dispassionate Texans, falter before the task of describing Texas. Like Alaska, it is a separate kingdom, enormous, contradictory, overwhelming, a superstate of wealth, power, beauty, myth, abundance (and disappointing stretches of barrenness). There are those who love Texas and those who despise it blindly, but no traveler has ever been indifferent to it.

Texas has birthed so many legends that a separate category of American literature can safely be devoted to the state, and the style known as "Texan" (and not even a Texan can adequately define it) has reached to the far corners of the world. Texas equals super: everything in Texas is just bigger and bolder and perhaps even more imaginative than anywhere else in the American continent, and most Americans, however reluctantly, appear to accept Texas in its heroic posture.

Perhaps an outsider, unprejudiced and with a dash of humor, can best see Texas, and it is the distinguished Irish storyteller and American traveler Sean O'Faolain on whom falls the burden of getting to the roots of the superstate. Here are his thoughts:

"Most areas in the world may be placed in latitude and longitude, described chemically in their earth, sky and water, rooted and fuzzed over with identified flora and peopled with known fauna, and there's an end to it. Then there are others where fable, myth, preconception, love, longing or prejudice step in and so distort a cool, clear appraisal that a kind of high-colored magical confusion takes permanent hold. Greece is such an area, and those parts of England where King Arthur walked. One quality of such places as I am trying to define is that a very large part of them is personal and subjective. And surely Texas is such a place.

"I have moved over a great part of Texas and I know that within its borders I have seen just about as many kinds of country, contour, climite and conformation as there are in the world, saving only the Arctic, and a good north wind can even bring the icy breath down. The stern, horizon-fenced plains of the Panhandle are foreign to the little wooded hills and sweet streams in the Davis Mountains. The rich citrus orchards of the Rio Grande Valley do not relate to the sagebrush grazing of South Texas. The hot and humid air of the Gulf Coast has no likeness in the cool crystal in the northwest of the Panhandle. And Austin on its hills among the bordered lakes might be across the world from Dallas.

"What I am trying to say is that there is no physical or geographical unity in Texas. Its unity lies in the mind. And this is not only in the Texan mind. The word Texas becomes a symbol to everyone in the world. There's no question that this Texas of fable is often synthetic, sometimes untruthful, and often romantic, but that in no way diminishes its strength as a symbol."

Variety, contradictions, idiosyncracies: former President Johnson on the banks of the Pedernales, shaded with live oaks; the astounding open ranges of the world-famous King ranch; oil derricks and natural gas; green belts of wheat and long, dreary open roads; the dusty and wind-torn Panhandle; the sandy hills around Monahans, the shadowy pines and rice fields behind the Gulf of Mexico; the very modern city of Houston, the state's largest, on the Gulf Coast plain, northwest of Galveston Bay; the Staked Plains of the western Panhandle, scene of the far-roaming Comanches, cattle rustlers, and Mexican bandits; up beyond the Rio Grande in country cut by gorge and canyon and covered with mesquite, stunted oak, huisache, chaparral and cenizo; the wild and mountainous regions beyond Big Bend National Park, Texas' only all-American preserve. Beyond the semicircular escarpment west of Waco, Austin (the state capital), and San Antonio (the prettiest city), spreads truly picturesque Texas, with its ghosts of cowboy tradition and early ranch history; its memories of longhorns on their springtime journey up the long, long trail to Kansas and Montana, and of spurred and jingling riders peering through dust-battered eyes at the glare of far horizons.

Texas isn't a state—it's an empire, as a former mayor of Dallas once said with the true Texas flourish. The myth that it is one vast, blank, gray, dusty, monotonous state of uniformity is denied both by an American, John Steinbeck, and by O'Faolain, who has this to say about the non-TV meaning of Texas:

"Nature here is endlessly inventive. Even if one has no special interest in farming or folklore, bird life or plant life, Texas instantaneously evokes one's curiosity about such things and keeps it on the alert: as when we discover, for example, that the political, social, and even military history of Texas has grown with the very grass—the food of the bison on whose flesh the original nomad Comanches and Apaches lived—and that in the end the Indians were beaten out of their sheltering plains and hills not by rifles turned against them but against the wandering buffalo. It was with the decimation of the buffalo that the Indian menace began to wilt and old strong points like Fort Griffin became ghost towns, their work done. But empires fade and grass still grows. It went on nourishing those later ruminants of the prairies, the longhorns of the great ranches."

Cotton and cattle, mesquite and cactus, tall gums and myrtle, cedar-darkened and laurel-sheened hills, the green of corn and the green of grass, bluebonnets and maguey, arid wastes and yielding fertility; widespread variety, dramatic contrasts, the strange contradictions of an empire eight hundred miles wide, with 170 million acres, two hundred and fifty-four counties—size of a mind-shaking hugeness. Not even a Texan can possibly know more than a handful of his own turf. It is simply too big.

The variety of Texas extends also to its cities and major towns—Galveston, Brownsville, Amarillo, Waco, Midland, El Paso, Fort Worth—each bearing out its regional nature, and to its competitive giants, Dallas and Houston. They are both urban dynamos: Dallas oriented toward business and finance (and still hypersensitive about its reputation for violence), Houston enjoying its role as the petroleum capital of America. They are both spawns of post-World War II America, the new Horatio Alger cities, moneyed and magnetic to the ambitious American, breeding their own cultures and mores in the flatness of the Southwest; cities from which will emerge tomorrow's social and economic and political power.

The Texas of legend, of tradition, of truth, of the nostalgia that every American would love to accept for his own, that pierces deep into the psyche of the native Texan who believes it wholeheartedly, the Texas that was at the core of the teaching of the noted English scholar and Texan, Gil Dobie, the Texas that still clutches at the imagination is what Sean O'Faolain unforgettably illuminates:

"The symbol of the old true Texan tradition is the remote cowboy and *vaquero* with his lonely, passionate, arrogant rejection of the ways of the busy world. The frontier, the ranches, the prairies, the dusty trails, the wide spaces under the lofty stars, the unending struggle between man and nature have bred a stubborn individualism, an admiration for every kind of personal skill, self-reliance and unconventionality, bred their own tempo, their own humor, their own heroism. They have bred a real culture in T. S. Eliot's definition of the word— i.e., a complete life mode; not something to be hung on the wall like a picture or an antique, but life as it is lived, fully and skillfully. . . . Within that old frontier way of life men could enjoy the luxury of being persons; they could be different; they did not have to be buttons out of a button mold. They were sometimes interesting, sometimes what we call colorful, sometimes gaudy, and on special occasions they could perform gestures splendid enough for an old saga.''

In parts of Texas, under the endless skies, on the great plains, thousands of unheralded cowpokes would like to feel they are still living out the legend—daily.

THE TRUE
SOUTHWEST

"This is the sense of the desert hills, that there is room enough and time enough," wrote Mary Austin of this glorious region, this glorious expanse of the United States: two states, one area, the old New Mexico Territory.

New Mexico
Arizona

Back in time, this elemental land was a province of Mexico; before that, a province of the Spanish colonial empire, as its architectural remains—particularly the Missions—proclaim. Still further back in time, it was the range of the Amerindians, whose descendants are still on the scene: the nomadic Navajos and Apaches, the Pueblos and Hopis and Zuñis and Papagos and Pimas and Yumas. During prehistoric years, the stone-and-adobe dwellings of the Indians were dotted throughout this raw-and-red land. The Southwest is an area that inspires crescendos of lyricism, such as those from the pen of Jack Schaefer:

"It is a land of infinite variety, holding within itself all the geographic zones of the continent. In a matter of hours you can leave a well-watered valley, move out over the desert zone, climb long rolling rises to the grassland, continue on up a mountain slope above the timber line to the bare lichen-marked rock, and at last on the highest peak find the eternal cold of the Arctic. And then, looking out from your arctic peak, you can see, far below, stretching away past vision, the dominant encompassing feature that gives unity to the region—the great arid distorted plains called deserts that the Indians found millennia ago and the Spaniards found four centuries ago and we Anglos are finding now.

"It is a land of natural wonders, lavish beyond any other region. Grand Canyon, Carlsbad Caverns, White Sands, Petrified Forest, Painted Desert, Sunset Crater, Organ Pipe, and saguaro cactus forests—these simply set the tone. The entire region abounds in twisted gorges and mystic badlands and weird spiny growths and strange-shaped soaring mesas and futuristic wind-sculptures in rock. It is a place where Nature has played artist on a grand scale through long geologic ages.

"It is a land of sky and sunlight and color. And the sky is not a sorry flattened overcast that hangs pressing on the earth, but a limitless depth of the very space in which the earth itself is poised. Deep blue over New Mexico, lighter blue over Arizona, it sweeps so vast over the distances that whole storms can be seen in their entirety scudding across it. . . . Sunlight is a living presence, more and purer and more golden than that of boasting Florida and California. There is a wide strip across the southern portion of both states which has sunlight 80 per cent of all daylight hours of the year. And this is sunlight in all its phases: a magic mantle over the land during the day, a miracle of luminance on the ridges and far mountains in late afternoon, a superb always-different panorama of color in the evening setting. . . . Color! Color is everywhere, the full range of the earth's palette, ever changing, always renewed. The Southwest is a place where Nature continues to play artist through every moment of every day.

"It is a land, too, that holds history in the palm of a huge protecting hand. Its high, dry climate preserves relics of the long past and adds through each successive epoch to its mighty outdoor museum of antiquities. The very poverty of its material resources permits the past to live on, little changed, into each new present."

The Southwest is a stunning compilation of the visual, the historic, the human, the poetic. Navajoland, the Canyon de Chelly, the Sangre de Cristo Mountains; adobes and cliff dwellings and ancient Aztec ruins; weird and dismaying forms of plant life; starkly sinister Penitente chapels on remote and lonely hilltops. The whole region is a mosaic of natural wonders. The supreme example, of course, is the Grand Canyon, impossible to describe and so often described in floods of words. An English writer, J. B. Priestley, perhaps understated it best in *The Grand Colorado; The Story of a River and Its Canyons:* "Those who have not seen it will not believe any possible description. Those who have seen it know that it cannot be described. . . . In fact, the Grand Canyon is a sort of landscape Day of Judgment. It is not a show place, a beauty spot, but a revelation. The Colorado River made it; but you feel when you are there that God gave the Colorado River its instructions."

Here also are Alamogordo, Los Alamos, and White Sands; jets, missiles, and rocketry; a measureless testing ground for tomorrow. Played off against the urgency of time and space (and the Southwest is space beyond belief) are the lasting innocent qualities of Santa Fe and Taos, the wise and reserved life style of the Navajos deep among the blood-red buttes and mesas and canyons of their protected territory. And the romantic Southwest of Billy the Kid and Wyatt Earp, of Apaches on the warpath, and of delicious legends (still alive!) of gold hidden deep in the Superstition Mountains of Arizona. It is the winding place of America's most romantic river, the Rio Grande, rising in Colorado, grandly sweeping over civilizations—from the Indian, Mexican, and Spanish to the interloper, the American, who dispossessed them all. It is arid land suddenly bursting with color where the river and irrigation come to its rescue. Water is the heartfelt worry of this region; water is precious and fought over. It is wilderness area, millions of acres of national forests, of wandering room, such as the great stretching grandeur of Pecos Wilderness, to please the most demanding Daniel Boone.

And it is desert, the wasteland, the sun-punished place. Of the beauty and mystery of the great desert of the Southwest, none has written with more feeling than John Steinbeck:

"At night in this waterless air the stars come down just out of reach of your fingers. In such a place lived the hermits of the early church piercing to infinity with unlittered minds. The great concepts of oneness and of majestic order seem always to be born in the desert. The quiet counting of the stars, and observation of their movements, came first from desert places. I have known desert men who chose their places with quiet and slow passion, rejecting the nervousness of a watered world. These men have not changed with the exploding times except to die and be replaced by others like them. . . .

"And there are true secrets in the desert. In the war of sun and dryness against living things, life has its secrets of survival. Life, no matter on what level, must be moist or it will disappear. I find most interesting the conspiracy of life in the desert to circumvent the death rays of the all-conquering sun. The beaten earth appears defeated and dead, but it only appears so. A vast and inventive organization of living matter survives by seeming to have lost. The gray and dusty sage wears oily armor to protect its inward small moistness. Some plants engorge themselves with water in the rare rainfall and store it for future use. Animal life wears a hard, dry skin or an outer skeleton to defy the desiccation. And every living thing has developed techniques for finding or creating shade. Small reptiles and rodents burrow or slide below the surface or cling to the shaded side of an outcropping. Movement is slow to preserve energy, and it is a rare

166

animal which can or will defy the sun for long. A rattlesnake will die in an hour of full sun. Some insects of bolder inventiveness have devised personal refrigeration systems. Those animals which must drink moisture get it at second hand—a rabbit from a leaf, a coyote from the blood of a rabbit.

"One may look in vain for living creatures in the daytime, but when the sun goes and the night gives consent, a world of creatures awakens and takes up its intricate pattern. Then the hunted come out and the hunters, and the hunters of the hunters. The night awakes to buzzing and to cries and barks.

"When, very late in the history of our planet, the incredible accident of life occurred, . . . a new thing emerged, soft and helpless and unprotected in the savage world of unlife. . . . The first life might easily have been snuffed out and the accident may never have happened again—but, once it existed, its first quality, its duty, preoccupation, direction, and end, shared by every living thing, is to go on living. And so it does and so it will until some other accident cancels it. And the desert, the dry and sun-lashed desert, is a good school in which to observe the cleverness and the infinite variety of techniques of survival under pitiless opposition. Life could not change the sun or water the desert, so it changed itself.

"The desert, being an unwanted place, might well be the last stand of life against unlife. . . . If the most versatile of living forms, the human, now fights for survival as it always has, it can eliminate not only itself but all other life. And if that should transpire, unwanted places like the desert might become the harsh mother of repopulation. For the inhabitants of the desert are well trained and well armed against desolation. Even our own misguided species might re-emerge from the desert. The lone man and his sun-toughened wife who cling to the shade in an unfruitful and uncoveted place might, with their brothers in arms—the coyote, the jackrabbit, the horned toad, the rattlesnake, together with a host of armored insects—these trained and tested fragments of life might well be the last hope of life against nonlife. The desert has mothered magic things before this."

THE PROMISED LAND

California

It is both fabulously beautiful and man-made ugly; it is hot and cold, wondrous and appalling, mountainous and bleakly empty; it is a state of majestic forests, rocky and beach-pretty coastline, fruitful valleys, gentle hills, lush greenness, and frightening desolation; a place of beautiful urban areas and billboard jungles. California is the best of America, the hideous worst of America; it is a state of extremes. No, it is not one state; there are three Californias. The late Eugene Burdick, scholar, historian, and novelist, bravely tried to encompass California into some manageable generalization:

"Even on a map the state looks odd. Four of the boundary lines are as straight as a surveyor's eye can make them. The fifth is the huge wriggling gorge that the Colorado has cut for itself. The sixth boundary is stupefying. It is the Pacific Ocean. The California Current and millions of years of savage storm waves and winds have worked at the western edge of California. This line is made up of jagged inlets, irregular sandbars, unlikely harbors, long white beaches. It changes constantly; every year some of the tall soft cliffs tumble into the ocean and part of California is gone. The upshot is a state that bulges forward and rests on a very narrow bottom. If it were detached from the rest of the United States it would slowly pivot on San Diego and fall into the Pacific Ocean. It is off-balance.

"Most states are fairly uniform in climate and terrain, and this tends to make their citizens somewhat similar. California has few uniformities—and fantastic differences. Part is white, hot desert, part perpetual snow, part subtropical and part heavily wooded with pine and oak and redwood. It has an active volcano. It has a place called Bagdad where a man looked into the sky for 767 days for rain and was rewarded by a touch of wet on the 768th day. This was the longest unofficially recorded dry period in America. But another man, at Hoegees Camp, stood unbelievingly as it rained twenty-six inches in a single day and watched the deluge melt mountains into soft mud. Huge redwoods slid down slick canyons, and enormous boulders came loose with a large suck and ponderously, surrounded by tons of mud, crashed down on the redwoods. Although the record books do not acknowledge it, this was the heaviest rainfall in a twenty-four-hour period in American history.

"The north is north of San Francisco. It is laced by rivers: the Mad, the Klamath, the Eel, the Russian. The rivers come down in hard blue currents, carving gorges out of rock, whipping around established and immovable mountains. The water is endless, blue and cold and very steady. The rivers tumble past towns like Redding, Eureka, Oroville, and Williams, and past vast reaches of firs, oaks, redwoods, and evergreens. Some of the towns were boom towns that decayed and almost disappeared and then came back strong, all in a hundred years. . . .

"In the south the beaches are broader and the cliffs are lower, and finally, around San Diego, they almost disappear. The ocean-water temperature rises. There is less fog, the winds are milder; there are more sharks and fewer crabs. The land becomes brown, the rainfall drops off, palm trees take the place of redwoods. The hills are beige and roll soft around towns like Santa Barbara and San Bernardino. And the hot white empty sands of Palm Springs and Indio and Twenty-Nine Palms are suddenly priceless because water has been brought in. The desert parts of the south would be grimly Saharan were it not for the long green lines of the aqueducts. With water added, the sands become lush and green but remain hot."

The city, of course, is San Francisco (not California's capital; inland Sacramento is), "a living fiction," the city that has earned the reputation of being every American's second city after his own home town. A blue-and-white city, fog washed, gleaming, rising splendidly on its hills, and with a small corner of China built in. San Francisco is the dream place on the Bay that "opens to the Pacific through a narrow gut created by some ancient seismic rupture," Burdick writes. "The sea flowed through the Golden Gate into what had been a large landlocked valley. Because the Bay is an accident, because it was occasioned by a tremendous fracture rather than the slow, symmetrical erosion of land by sea, it has a built-in, fundamental beauty." And the Golden Gate Bridge, the symbol and the promise, is the most beautiful bridge, probably, in America.

In its staggering diversity of natural endowments, California is practically a universe unto itself. The Sierra Nevada, the highest mountain range in the United States outside of Alaska; the lush wine-and-pasture land country of the Napa Valley and Sonoma County; the geometric agricultural patterns of the rich, yielding flat land of the Central Valley; the dead, planet-line contours of Death Valley; the lovely hills of Marin County; Monterey County (John Steinbeck country, the setting for his *Cannery Row* and *Tortilla Flat*) and the rocky Monterey Peninsula with picturesque Carmel (and well-tailored Pebble Beach); and below it, Point Lobos and the exciting wilderness of the Big Sur.

The park system includes wilderness and forest and wild beaches and bosky parks. Among the most famously beautiful are Yosemite, Kings Canyon, Sequoia National Park, and farther south, the Joshua Tree National Monument. And then there is the Mark Twain country with its faded mining camps and stories of wealth and the days of the Forty-Niners that California will never let die. How can this many-sided state be truly encompassed, or its problems solved? Will the Point Reyes National Seashore—fifty-three thousand acres of wild, wooded hills; grassy, treeless, windy tablelands; long, surf-whipped sand-dune beaches; chalky white cliffs—remain an entity without interference from developers? Water, pell-mell building, overgrazing, the threatened destruction of priceless stands of redwoods—these are only a handful of the crises that face California today. Yet it is startling fact, according to William O. Douglas, that the Federal Government owns 45 million of the 100 million acres within the state, "and the percentage will have to increase if the recreational needs of the twenty-first century are going to be met."

When Californians tire of their myriad problems, they get away, taking John Muir's advice, that they "climb the mountains and get their good tidings." The mountains are the Sierra, the great California wilderness, whose great vistas still feed the hungry vision. "In terms of geological time," reports Mary Carter, "the Sierra is young, with all the tumultuous exuberance and swings of adolescence in its moods and climates. In its deep valleys the air is tender and still; upon its high open reaches the sun rages like a storm and lightning makes the granite gong. Its western approaches are gradual and reflective; the eastern flank presents itself with mammoth suddenness, a sheer palisade of peaks heaved up from the valley floor. It is a fortress of lacy minarets and crenelated battlements. Though parts of it seethe underneath with volcanic energies, other areas of its surface look like that of a dead moon, raked and rubbled with boulders, a tundra so barren that living organisms must root in snow and so high that, stunned for oxygen, some imagine they can hear the whine of the jet stream. It is a gentle wilderness of gardens: Japanese, diminutive and exquisite with wild garlic and bonzai juniper; English, with stout grasses, daisies, columbine, perennial borders, larkspur; Swiss, with steep slopes of lupine and conifers; Himalayan, with thickets of azalea, rhododendron, creepers; desert, with succulents blooming suddenly and fiercely."

At the extreme other end of California—far back from Los Angeles, the teeming city of movie makers—is deathly quiet desert, the fierce and terrifying Death Valley, bordering on Nevada; the driest, the lowest, the hottest area in the Western Hemisphere. Death Valley names still send chills running down the spine: Badwater, Furnace Creek, Devil's Golf Course, Dante's View, Funeral Mountains, Coffin Canyon, Dead Man's Gulch, Funeral Mine. Now a national monument, once a place of "awful desolation," it is now a friendly valley, Jack Schaefer claims, that offers rewards of beauty and grandeur and solace.

"Death Valley. An apt name—from the point of view of white men who regarded this desert valley as an obstacle to be crossed or a region to be exploited for quick profit. Dig into the life and legend of the Panamint Indians, a branch of the Shoshone Nation. To them it was a death valley, too—but in another sense. They called it Tomesha, or Ground Afire. Again a neat name—from the white men's perspective of menace lurking in the land. Literally the word meant 'red paint' or 'red earth,' from a red pigment found in the valley and used in ceremonial painting. No hint of menace from the Indian point of view. To the Panamints it was a friendly valley. They lived with it, accepting its conditions, following the seasons from the warm valley depths in winter to the heights of the surrounding mountains in summer. Old tales persist that some of their camps in the valley were Indian health resorts, places where the sick and aged came for warmth in winter and the therapeutic sun in summer. Many of the aged died, but their deaths were not imposed by a harsh environment; rather, the warmth and serenity made their last days more enjoyable."

NORTHWEST...TO ALASKA, THE LAST WILDERNESS

In Oregon, Washington, and Alaska, the American wilderness is at last perceived—or at least enough wilderness, enough space, enough emptiness, and even desolation, to warm the spirit hungry for a personal encounter with nature. The Pacific Northwest (and throw in the uppermost counties of northern California, for good measure) is a vigorous area neither spoiled nor entirely tamed by man's instinctive effort to make himself comfortable. Here, for stretches of hundreds of miles, the wilderness prevails in awful triumph, the metamorphic rock and lava formations a reminder of the earth's considerable age, and of its tortured, slow development from the nightmare time before life stirred in the darkness.

The far, watery Northwest frontier: from the wheatlands of Washington, a plunge into the wild, green Cascade Range, over Snoqualmie Pass or through the Cascade Tunnel; a final emergence onto the lush slope facing Puget Sound, the setting sun, the broad, blue western sea—the Pacific, the wild part of the world, old enough and big enough to overshadow its own history. Calvin Kentfield writes that "the sea is a wilderness—a wilderness beating relentlessly on wilderness—and like the forest, it yields up riches for the civilized life. From the deep waters of the ocean, from the beds and shallows of Puget Sound, from the massive flow of the Great River (the Columbia) come tuna and salmon, oysters and crabs, shrimp and clams, for the canneries of Astoria, Willapa Bay, Vancouver, and the Inside Passage.

"Though most denizens of the Pacific Northwest seldom actually see the sea, it is ever-present in their lives. They may live and work on the sea's arms, on the straits of Georgia and Juan de Fuca, on Puget Sound and the Columbia estuary, but the brooding ocean itself is remote except to deep-sea fishermen and sailors. Sailors discovered the land, explored its waterways, named its places; sailors such as Captain Cook and George Vancouver, who sailed with Cook at the age of fourteen, circumnavigating the southern hemisphere and subsequently exploring the American Pacific Coast. As the country grew the sea took out furs and brought in merchandise, food and niceties from around the Horn; and it took the adventurous, the bored and the greedy to Alaska to search for gold or to unburden those who found it. Port Townsend at the head of Admiralty Inlet, the main channel to Seattle and Tacoma, was the first port of entry on the West Coast, and as late as 1908 its exports were valued at much more than those of any other American port on the Pacific. It's nearly a ghost town now."

A terrain of spectacular rocky promontories along the brink of the continent; rain country; forest country; chilled mists; heavenly agricultural valleys; of mountains, great

Oregon
Washington

171

mountains such as Hood in Oregon, and the queen of American peaks, Rainier, in Washington.

The main cities, in Oregon, are Portland, the largest by far, a deep water port near the junction of the Willamette and Columbia rivers; Salem, the capital of the state, some thirty-five miles south of Portland; and Eugene, still farther up the Willamette. In Washington, Spokane lies at the east, near the Idaho border; Tacoma and Olympia, the capital, in the west on the waters that lead out to the Pacific.

In contrast to the cities, there is wilderness. "On the Olympic Peninsula in Washington," Calvin Kentfield says, "the wilderness stands unchanged since the first dawn. On the windward side of the mountains, 150 inches of rain will fall in an average year, and these primitive rainforests are rank and dark, full of wild beasts and twenty-foot ferns that grow in Pleistocene silence from the forest floor.

"The Olympic Mountains, a miniature Himalaya, rise sharp and snow-capped from the center of this low arboreal jungle. Saturated clouds obscure the peaks a good part of the year, casting a mood of Kierkegaardian introspection over the entire massif. You could circle the peninsula for days on end and never know those mountains were there, yet sometimes they will stand out crisp and wild from the sea."

A country of bleak, rocky, and treacherous headlands; of fogs and sea lions; timber and logging country; shrouded lighthouses; of tall, plummeting waterfalls; aromatic beech and birch woods; romantic promontories exposing vistas of a veiled and craggy gorge that could be the setting for a Wagnerian opera—the mighty Columbia River, the "Great River" of the early explorers Lewis and Clark, John Day, George Vancouver. "It was the Oregon of the ambitious and adventurous people who followed the famous trail across the plains," again writes Kentfield:

"Now the Columbia is a commercial thoroughfare of vast international importance, and if you follow it upstream toward The Dalles, you will see its banks change before your eyes in a few minutes, from the lush, rain-blessed slopes of the windward side of the mountains to the sere plateau. It's like moving from the Garden into the desert wilderness."

Sea and forest, watery world, fresh and salt; and the abundant Willamette Valley, between the mountain ranges, a rich land and a relief from the precipitous, craggy surroundings. Rainier appears, in full view from bustling Portland. It is described by Kentfield: "The air now was a desert air, not a cloud, not a trace of haze, a rare magnificent day in the Pacific Northwest. All the dazzling white volcanoes stood out against the enameled blue sky—Mount Hood, highest mountain in Oregon, close as the hand in front of your face; Mount Adams, glacial, blunt, its top blown off in some vast prehistoric explosion, rising more than 12,000 feet from rugged, roughly accessible wilds north of the river; Mount St. Helena to the left, a pyramid as perfect and pure as Fujiyama; and The Mountain itself, diminished by the curve of the earth but clearly visible over the shoulder of St. Helena—all cold members of the Circle of Fire, titans of a wild country."

The late Jack Kerouac, hobo, roamer, the guru of the Beat Generation, wrote, "No man should go through life without once experiencing healthy, even bored solitude in the wilderness, finding himself depending solely on himself and thereby learning his true and hidden strength. Learning, for instance, to eat when he's hungry and sleep when he's sleepy."

Kerouac once spent an entire summer alone as a fire lookout on a mountaintop in the High Cascades—"under the pure, cloud-capped sparkling skies of the Northwest. . . . Here for the first time you're high enough really to begin to see the Cascades. Dazzles of light to the north show where Ross Lake sweeps back all the way to Canada, opening a view of the Mt. Baker National Forest as spectacular as any vista in the Colorado Rockies."

The mountain that was Kerouac's home was appropriately named Desolation Peak, and in this rain-soaked, misty, wild setting he watched for fires and surveyed a panorama of beauty that few Americans since the redoubtable John Muir have been privileged to enjoy—alone. The life cycle of raw nature inflicts an inevitable mystical vision:

"In the red dusk, the mountains were symphonies in pink snow . . . Jack Mountain, Three Fools Peak, Freezeout Peak, Golden Horn, Mt. Terror, Mt. Fury, Mt. Despair, Crooked Thumb Peak, Mt. Challenger, and the incomparable Mt. Baker, bigger than the world in the distance. . . . Pink snow and the clouds all distant and frilly like ancient remote cities of Buddhaland splendor, and the wind working incessantly— whish, whish—booming. . . . I could see the firs reflected in the moonlit lake five thousand feet below, upside down, pointing to infinity. . . . And all the insects ceased in honor of the moon. . . . Sixty-three sunsets I saw revolve on that perpendicular hill . . . mad raging sunsets pouring in sea foams of cloud through unimaginable crags like the crags you grayly drew in pencil as a child, with every rose tint of hope beyond, making you feel just like them, brilliant and bleak beyond words."

And then were was the bear, the unseen presence of primitive life, the end-of-summer terror felt but never glimpsed, the stuffed plaything of childhood, the looming menace of forest where man dares intrude because he cannot help himself:

"One morning I found bear stool and signs of where the monster had taken a can of frozen milk and squeezed it in his paws and bit into it with one sharp tooth, trying to suck out the paste. In the foggy dawn I looked down on the mysterious Ridge of Starvation with its fog-lost firs and its hills humping into invisibility, and the wind blowing the fog by like a faint blizzard, and I realized that somewhere in the fog stalked the bear.

"And it seemed, as I sat there, that this was the Primordial Bear, and he owned all the Northwest and all the snow and commanded all the mountains. He was King Bear, who could crush my head in his paws and crack my spine like a stick, and this was his house, his yard, his domain. Though I looked all day, he would not show himself in the mystery of those silent foggy slopes. He prowled at night among unknown lakes, and in the early morning the pearl-pure light that shadowed mountainsides of fir made him blink with respect. He had milleniums of prowling here behind him. He had seen the Indians and the Redcoats come and go, and he would see much more. He continuously heard the reassuring rapturous rush of silence, except when near creeks; he was aware of the light material the world is made of, yet he never discoursed, nor communicated by signs, nor wasted a breath complaining; he just nibbled and pawed, and lumbered along snags paying no attention to things inanimate or animate. His big mouth chew-chewed in the night, I could hear it across the mountain in the starlight. Soon he would come out of the fog, huge, and come and stare in my window with big burning eyes. He was Avalokiteshvara the Bear, and his sign was the gray wind of autumn.

"I was waiting for him. He never came."

And so to the last remaining American frontier, where Nature can afford to be wasteful; it is the territory beyond—of snow mountains and glaciers, of driving rain, carpeted greenness, Indians living out their tireless rhythms of an old life, fantastic marine life, and of the Yukon and tales of Robert W. Service and gold somewhere, out there even beyond.

Alaska is the land of the ice age: the gray mass of Mendenhall Glacier, striped with

Alaska

ice green, patched red with the ubiquitous firewood, broad and white-shouldered with its dazzling snowfields. Between the Chilkat Range and the Kakunau Mountains, one witnesses an unearthly world, according to a mesmerized John Dos Passos:

"We are entering the Ice Age. Here glaciers still carve out the valleys. With your own eyes you can detect the piling up of moraines. The streams that gush, gray with rock flour, from under the ice, wind and wander over plains of broken stones. Some day they may dig themselves beds and become rivers. Now they are mere torrents that flood the land in the spring thaw. Water pours from sievelike cliffs. The grinding weight of the ice and the rush of thawed water toward the sea is fashioning these gorges. Escarpments stand up raw and new. Between snowfields, seamed and splintered by frost and storm, the rock ridges strain toward the sky. It is a land in the agony of creation. . . .

". . . you feel a belly-knotting excitement in the unfolding of peaks and snowfields. Terror, perhaps. The hackles tingle. Life has little part in this landscape. Stunted spruces cling to the lower buttresses, a few alders and dwarf willows grow in the sheltered hollows. There are moss and lichen on the slopes, enough Arctic herbiage here and there to support a few mountain sheep, enough berries and wild pea vines to feed an occasional bear. No trails. No sign of human habitation. Through the centuries Athabaskan hunting parties have camped on the shores; in more recent years an occasional prospector searching the rock with hammer and chisel for gold-bearing ore, has labored up the frosted valleys. Captain Cook noted the vast terror of these mountains. They are out of human scale. A man is struck with the sort of awe Ezekiel the priest felt when, standing among the captives by the river of Chebar, he saw fiery wheels in that whirlwind that came out of the north."

The territory beyond is a land of thousands of lakes and ponds, magnificent views beyond the counting, broad valleys, a dozen Switzerlands piled together; the silvery reaches of bays, a glacier called Malaspina the size of Rhode Island, skies that stretch to the far, far horizon, bears munching on leaves beside a paved highway, stands of Douglas fir, jade-green waters—the cornucopia of lavished nature to the north.

If the mountain is the American symbol of attainment and pleasure—something to climb, to stare at, to brood upon, to lift the eyes to—then Alaska has the giant, Mount McKinley. John Dos Passos saw it at daybreak:

"The valley where I stood was still blue-dark; the sunrise was hidden by the low mountains that hemmed us in. Suddenly the great 20,000-foot peak glowed like a hot coal through the clouds. The peak, with its great curved ridges rising to a sharp-cut pyramid of snow, shone out for a moment in the horizontal sunlight.

"It was a morning of marvelous sights: grizzly bears strolling among the berry bushes on the rough slopes; a golden eagle and nineteen Dall sheep; a magnificent red fox at eye level, staring from a washout in the wall of the gulch; twenty-two caribou on the ridge, rearing their great antlers against the clouds; a flock of willow ptarmigan, their feathers already tipped with white for the winter; a pair of huge bull moose lumbering about in the shrubby growth that was all yellow and orange and red. . . ."

Alaska, as Dos Passos rightly claims, is now the great show of America. Its towns —Juneau and Fairbanks and Skagway, for example—hum with the kind of spirit that recalls Gold Rush days, and its villages and underdeveloped areas are beginning to fill with the brand of American whose eyes have always sought a far horizon. Its new oil boom will take this glacial territory to the high fever whose accompanying symptoms are desperate hard work and prizes beyond the telling. It will be the next explosion in the legend of America—where, with luck and grit, anything will be possible in a territory whose natural wealth awaits the explorer, the visionary, and the fervent conservationist, all of whom will play out their traditional roles.

174

THE ISLAND PARADISE

"The most improbable state in the Union," Robert Carson wrote, "consists of twenty volcanic peaks that stick up out of the middle of the Pacific Ocean. They are well over two thousand miles from the rest of the Republic, and their next-closest neighbor is little Midway, more than a thousand miles to the West. Only seven of these isolated volcanic islands are inhabited. But the charismatic effect of Hawaii on the rest of America and the world is out of all proportion to its size and relatively remote location."

Captain Cook, Polynesia, New England missionaries, subtropical and tropical vegetation, splendid beaches, lush landscapes, pineapple and sugar plantations, warm salt water, endlessly shining sun, fair trade winds, volcanic eruptions, blue-water lagoons, sweet waterfalls, rain forests, palms. Any evocation of Hawaii, where it is always late spring, inevitably reads like a travel folder, and in truth Hawaii is now literally America's playground. Its surfing, such as at Sunset Beach and Waimea Bay, is perhaps unrivaled. Few traces of authentic Polynesian life remain; commerce and tourism prevail and the charm is rapidly fading. Honolulu (on Oahu Island) is sadly overrun, but considerable beauty still remains in the Outer Islands.

The islands are Kauai, Maui, Hawaii, and Molokai, prettily named, congenially different in texture and topography. Kauai is perhaps the dreamiest, thinly settled, with Oriental landscapes of rice paddies and taro patches, remote valleys and empty canyons —James Michener country—and the unscalable cliffs of Napali and the sinister canyon of Waimea, where mountain goats claw at the tops of ridges. Drops of four thousand feet and abysmal crevices are commonplace, and a preposterous swamp is situated on the crest of the mountains, fed by rainfall averaging four hundred and eighty inches a year—the wettest spot on the globe.

Maui is thickly vegetative in its interior, less glamorous and drier than Kauai, and at its eastern end, at Hana and Hamoa, reminiscent of an older and more leisurely Hawaii. The Iao Valley is blissfully unspoiled and the Haleakala Crater, ten thousand feet high, is a dramatic example of volcanic activity in the Islands. Maui's beaches can be touristy and appalling.

Hawaii, the Big Island, is geographically the most interesting of all the islands. Its four thousand square miles have wide variations in climate and topography. It has America's remotest national park, fields of orchids, tree-fern forests and falls, tremendous ranch lands, volcanoes, snow-capped mountains, deserts, white and black sand beaches; and it is the fishing grounds for wahoo, tuna, marlin, and mahimahi. Deep in its interior is adventure, beckoning space for the seekers of aloneness and primitive nature. The island is munificently spacious, completely undersettled, and impossible to spoil completely.

Molokai, best known for the leper colonies and the heroic endeavors of Father Damien, was once the secret isle of Hawaii—remote, unspoiled, little visited, empty. For a brief time, it is still what Hawaii was thirty years ago. The precipitous Pali coast, virginal tropic valleys, sylvan views, pineapples growing in the red earth, and deer, boar, and wild goats in the forests: These remain of an island, primitive and forgotten, that now sounds to the roar of the bulldozer as the old earth is torn up. When Molokai, developed and tarted up, receives the new invaders, the precious Polynesian quality of Hawaii will remain only in myth and memory.

Acknowledgments
(Continued from copyright page)

All articles quoted in the text originally appeared in *Holiday* and are reprinted here with their special permission, and with the permission of the following:

BRANDT & BRANDT: From "Idaho" by A. B. Guthrie, Jr., Copyright 1954 by the Curtis Publishing Company. From "Montana" by A. B. Guthrie, Jr., Copyright © 1965 by the Curtis Publishing Company. From "Wyoming" by Bernard De Voto, Copyright 1951 by the Curtis Publishing Company. From "Great Salt Lake" by Wallace Stegner, Copyright © 1957 by the Curtis Publishing Company. CURTIS BROWN, LTD.: From "Three Californias" by Eugene Burdick, Copyright © 1965 by the Curtis Publishing Company. From "Continental Divide" by Neil Morgan, Copyright © 1967 by the Curtis Publishing Company. From "Texas" by Sean O'Faolain, Copyright © 1958 by the Curtis Publishing Company. JOHN DOS PASSOS: From "Alaska" by John Dos Passos, Copyright © 1966 by the Curtis Publishing Company. FADIMAN ASSOCIATES, LTD.: From "Literature of the Rockies" by Clifton Fadiman, Copyright © 1963 by the Curtis Publishing Company. INTERNATIONAL FAMOUS AGENCY, INC.: From "Nevada Desert" by Walter van Tilburg Clark, Copyright © 1957 by the Curtis Publishing Company. THE STERLING LORD AGENCY: From "The Cascades" by Jack Kerouac, Copyright © 1958 by Jack Kerouac. HAROLD MATSON COMPANY, INC.: From "Pacific Northwest" by Calvin Kentfield, Copyright © 1962 by the Curtis Publishing Company. From "Dakota" by Jack Schaefer, Copyright 1955 by the Curtis Publishing Company. From *My Southwest* by Jack Schaefer, Copyright © 1959 by Jack Schaefer. MCINTOSH AND OTIS, INC.: From "Nebraska" by Mari Sandoz, Copyright © 1956 by the Curtis Publishing Company. DEBS MYERS: From "Kansas" by Debs Myers, Copyright 1951 by the Curtis Publishing Company. From "Colorado" by Debs Myers, Copyright © 1965 by the Curtis Publishing Company. RANDOM HOUSE, INC.: From "Mississippi" by William Faulkner, Copyright 1954 by William Faulkner. A revised version of this essay appears in *Big Woods* by William Faulkner. RUSSELL & VOLKENING, INC.: From "Illinois" by Saul Bellow, Copyright © 1957 by the Curtis Publishing Company. From "Everglades" by Benedict Thielen, Copyright © 1961 by the Curtis Publishing Company. THE VIKING PRESS, INC., AND WILLIAM HEINEMANN, LTD.: From *Travels with Charley in Search of America* by John Steinbeck. Copyright © 1961, 1962 by the Curtis Publishing Company, Inc., Copyright © 1962 by John Steinbeck.